THE AWESOME POWER OF THE LISTENING HEART

THE AWESOME POWER OF THE LISTENING HEART

JOHN W. DRAKEFORD

Zondervan Publishing House
Grand Rapids, Michigan

THE AWESOME POWER OF THE LISTENING HEART

© Copyright 1982 by The Zondervan Corporation,
Grand Rapids, Michigan.

Zondervan Publishing House,
1415 Lake Drive, S.E.,
Grand Rapids, Michigan 49506

Library of Congress Cataloging in Publication Data

Drakeford, John W.
 The awesome power of the listening heart.

 1. Listening. I. Title.
BF323.L5D73   1982   153.6   82-17518
ISBN 0-310-70261-5

All rights reserved. Printed in the United States of America. No part of this book may be used or reproduced in any manner whatsoever without written permission, except in the case of brief quotations embodied in critical articles and reviews.

Printed in the United States of America

84 85 86 87 88 89 90 / 10 9 8 7 6 5 4 3

Contents

Preface 9
1 The Most Underrated of All Sensory
 Experiences 13

What a Listening Skill Can Give You

2 A Valuable Educational Tool 21
3 A Resource for Helping Others 25

Three Superlatives in Changing Behavior

4 The Greatest of All Gifts 35
5 A Disease of Epidemic Proportions 43
6 Cruel and Unusual Punishment 47

Listening Levels

7 Eye-listening 59
8 Ear-listening 67
9 Head-listening 75
10 Hand-listening 81
11 Tactile-listening 87
12 Third-ear-listening 95
13 Body-listening 101

Targets for Listening Skills

14 The Public Relations Technique Nobody
 Mentions 109
15 A Forgotten Factor in Leadership 115
16 New Medicine for Sick Marriages 127

Mastering the Art of Listening

17 Understanding Fallacies About Listening ..139
18 Listening Inertia 143
19 Listening for the Sound of Silence 151
20 Asking Questions—Carefully 157
21 Avoiding Common Traps 165
22 Be Sure to Catch the Balloons 173

The author and publisher express appreciation for use of the following copyrighted materials:

"Listening Fosters Creativity," *American Way* (Aug. 1980).
Helen Keller, *Teacher: Anne Sullivan Macy* (Garden City, NY: Doubleday Co., Inc., © 1955).
The World Book Encyclopedia (Chicago: Field Enterprises Corporation, © 1964).
Helen Keller, *The Story of My Life* (New York: Doubleday, Doran and Co., Inc., 1933).
H. A. Brill, *Fundamental Conceptions of Psychoanalysis* (New York: Harcourt Brace and Co., Inc., 1921).
Newsweek (Dec. 1, 1980).
Hara Estroff Marano, "The Bonding of Mothers and Babies," *Smithsonian* (Feb. 1981).
Charles Spurgeon, *Lectures to My Students* (New York: Sheldon & Co., n.d.)
Whittaker Chambers, *Witness* (New York: Random House, © 1952 by Whittaker Chambers).
Ralph G. Nichols and Leonard A. Stevens, *Are You Listening?* (New York: McGraw-Hill Book Co., Inc., © 1957).
James J. Lynch, *The Broken Heart* (New York: Basic Book, Inc., © 1977).
Us (Apr. 14, 1981).
"The Other Dolly Parton," *McCall's* (Feb. 1981).
Nardi Reeder Campion, "Ask, Don't Tell," *Christian Herald* (Aug. 1966, © 1966 by Christian Herald Assn., Inc.).
Nehemia Curnock, Ed., *The Journal of Rev. John Wesley, A.M.* (London: The Epworth Press, 1909).
Dale Carnegie, *How to Win Friends and Influence People* (New York: Simon and Schuster, 1937).
"Lending an Ear," *Time* (Dec. 7, 1981).
Norman Rockwell, "My Adventures as an Illustrator," *Saturday Evening Post* (Apr. 2, 1960).
Time (Oct. 26, 1981).
Theodor Reik, *Listening with the Third Ear* (New York: Grove Press, Inc., 1955).
"West Point: The Silencing," *Newsweek* (June 18, 1973.)
Frank Capra, *The Name Above the Title* (New York: The Macmillan Co., copyright © 1971 by Frank Capra).
Portions of chapter 16 are excerpted from *Marriage: How to Keep a Good Thing Growing* by John W. Drakeford © 1979 by Impact Books.

Scripture quotations are from the following versions:

HOLY BIBLE, *New International Version*, copyright © 1978, New York Bible Society. Used by permission.
The Living Bible, copyright © 1971 by Tyndale House Publishers, Wheaton, IL. Used by permission.
The New English Bible. Copyright © The Delegates of the Oxford University Press and the Syndics of the Cambridge University, 1961, 1970. Reprinted by permission.

Preface

On one occasion, Helen Keller, who was both deaf and blind, was asked the ridiculous question: "If you could have either hearing or sight, which would you prefer?"

Her answer was, "Hearing." The surprise of her questioner, and of most people who consider the subject, is an indication of the scant consideration we give to the listening experience.

Listening is the most underrated of all the sensory experiences. One of the reasons for this is the failure of most people to appreciate the many facets of listening. Listening is a multidimensional skill, through which we gain information from the world around us, are able to help and reach out to others in a multitude of ways, and in the most elevated of uses, discover God.

Psychologists speak about the principle of parsimony—using the simplest skills that produce results. Complex procedures are used only after the more elementary have been demonstrated as inadequate. Listening is probably our best single example of applying the principle of parsimony to education and counseling and motivational procedures.

In many ways listening may be an answer to the plea of humans who want to devise an elementary skill by which life can be lived. If I were to announce there were one simple interpersonal skill which, if mastered, would make the possessor a well-informed, knowledgeable individual; a wiser person; a more desirable companion; a more effective husband or wife, father or mother, son or daughter; a better communicator; a counselor *par excellence;* a more skillful administrator, I would be besieged by requests to reveal it. And *listening* is that skill.

But what is the meaning of the term "listening heart?"

The figurative use of the word *heart* in our language shows that we often intuitively feel there is a part of the human functioning that is not recognized by the scientific fraternity. Our vocabulary includes phrases like *broken heart, heartsick, heartless, sweetheart.* When a worker slows down at his job, we sometimes say, "His heart is not in it." Or when he struggles with a difficult situation we urge him to "take heart."

Preeminently the heart is associated with the concept of love. I once visited a very nice holiday resort in the mountains of Brazil. Though I found it impossible to understand the Portuguese language, I was reminded that love is the universal language, for drawn on the inside of closet doors in the chalet where I was staying were the familiar hearts and arrows, bearing strange-looking names. Later in this volume we will see the way in which the message of love is conveyed by attention—which is generally indicated by listening.

Amid the spate of books on the subject of the human heart appeared a volume with a most unlikely title—*The Broken Heart*. The simple thesis of this book, written by a clinical psychologist, was that among the factors that go into the physical failure of a heart, the most important might be a psychological factor—loneliness.

Before you begin to complain about the poetic metaphor of the heart, let us notice that a number of behavioral scientists have used the equally lyrical metaphors about listening. Theodor Reik has advanced the anatomically impossible idea of listening with the third ear, by which an individual is able to perceive what is said, thought, and felt, as well as the voice within himself. Dominick Barbara has developed the idea of holistic listening, a process by which a person is able, in the words of Heraclitis, to "listen to the essence of things."

But holistic listening is more than this. When we involve the total organism, then we have achieved the ultimate in caring—listening with the heart.

Unique to this volume are "Listening Levels," in which eye-, ear-, head-, tactile-, third-ear-, body-, and heart-listening are discussed. For the author it was delightful insight and I hope it will be equally captivating for the reader.

This volume will help anyone who wants to launch himself on a venture of influencing, helping, and motivating his fellowman to discover *The Awesome Power of the Listening Heart*.

1
The Most Underrated of All Sensory Experiences

"Go to the house of God . . . to listen . . . Do not be quick with your mouth, . . . let your words be few"
(Eccl. 5:1–2 NIV).

What is the most important thing you do? If your work is people-centered, it will probably involve listening. Most professional and semi-professional people are faced with clients who ostensibly come to them for consultation, but as much as anything else, need a listening ear.

The lawyer, in the discussion of legal intricacies, finds his client anxious to recount the background information. Particularly in divorce proceedings the client is in emotional turmoil engendered by the events leading to the marital rupture and has a deep need to tell someone about it all.

A doctor seeing patients in his office frequently discovers that their bodies speak for themselves in "organ language." It has been estimated that 50 percent or more of the patients who seek a physician's services have nothing physically wrong with them. In discussing an obvious functional illness, the lid of the patient's seething cauldron of hostility, resentment, or self-pity may be opened. What should the physician do? Will he attempt to soothe with tranquilizers, refer the patient to a psychiatrist, or listen with one eye on the clock, all the while haunted by a vision of a crowded waiting room?

A nurse who works around a sick person for a long period of time grows increasingly familiar. As the patient's confidence in her grows, he may want to talk. The patient's weakness and uncertainty can cause him to interpret illness as a punishment. When he is ready to bare his soul, he apprehensively gestures for the nurse's listening ear.

The pastor frequently sees his church work as expressive communication—preaching or giving devotional talks to civic clubs—and fails to realize that many modern-day people long for his listening ear. In fact, the majority of his church members would be delighted if their pastor would organize his time to provide for the vital ministry of listening.

Rather unfortunately, he has not always been adequately prepared for this task. Much of his theological training has been aimed at intellectualizing theological concepts. A major portion of his practical preparation has been concerned with learning to project himself and express his thoughts with clarity and persuasiveness. But he's often much too busy with the mechanics of church life to spend time at listening!

I chanced to pick up a book in the home of a friend. The book, called *The Listener,* was inscribed:

> To my preacher,
> With deepest gratitude for being
> my "listener" in my hour of need.

Reading that statement, I felt not a little envious of this minister and the way he was perceived by his parishioner. It was one of the highest compliments any church member could pay a pastor.

Listening is the supreme communication skill, the top-line administrative technique, the salient counseling method, the key to conversation, the primary motivational technique—but it is generally overlooked.

Why is listening the Cinderella of the interpersonal skills? The primary reason is its difficulty.

One of the best examples of the principles and problems of communication is that most fundamental technique of moving messages which we call the Morse code. The code is the essence of simplicity, consisting of two sounds, *dit* and *dah.*

The sender, using a telegraph key, closes and opens a circuit, sending *dits* and *dahs* heard by the receiver. It is a beautiful illustration of the communication processes of encoding—as messages are put into *dits* and *dahs*—and decoding—as *dahs* and *dits* are translated by the receiver into the written language.

Despite all the assurances of how easy it is to learn Morse code, it can be exceedingly difficult. To obtain a radio operator's general license, the candidate must be able to send and receive the code at thirteen words per minute. When the Federal Communications Commission examiner tests a candidate, he simply monitors his ability to *receive* the code at thirteen words per minute. The assumption is that if one can receive messages at that speed he will certainly be able to transmit them at that speed. No test, therefore, is given for the ability to *send* messages.

The Morse code testing procedures highlight the one great principle of human-to-human communication—*it is much easier to send than to receive.*

A hopeful operator would have to be very foolish to spend all his time practicing sending skills. It would make much more sense for him to launch a major effort in improving his receiving ability. Likewise, success is never gained by a communicator who merely wants to use expressive communications skills. He must learn the assimilative communication skills if he is to gain information. Like the would-be Morse code operator, the aspiring listener must prepare himself for the discipline for which it calls.

Referring to listening as a "simple" skill does not recognize the fact that it often seems counter to all our natural tendencies. Listening means we have to focus on someone else; and many who do practice listening skills see them as a means to an end. As one observer noted about another individual, the only time he listens is when he himself is speaking.

Listening may be the most unselfish of all activities. It starts with Jesus' difficult command to His followers, "Let him deny himself" (Matt. 16:24).

The self-discipline required for listening is typical of all artistic endeavors. *Listening is an art.* Keep this in mind if you aspire to be a competent listener.

To the casual observer, it may seem that the artist's effortless achievements are simply native gifts. However, while artists are undoubtedly born, not made, they are certainly not born *made.* Years of observation, study, and hard work lie behind the smooth performance. Laborious hours have polished the rough hewn crystalline carbon of capacity until it shines in all its multifaceted diamond brilliance.

There is no easy pathway to the goal of effective listening. Once we accept the proposition that listening is an art, we must realize that it may require as much time, effort, and perseverance as painting, ballet, music, or any other of the art forms.

Convinced? Make up your mind to let nothing

keep you from mastering this art. Consider how valuable this skill will be in all that you do! Resolutely discipline yourself and launch into an enterprise that may revolutionize your life.

In the next segment of this book we will consider some of the objectives that can be obtained when you master listening skills.

What a Listening Skill Can Give You

2
A Valuable Educational Tool

Those who learn to listen, listen to learn. —J.W.D.

As part of a battery of listening tests, participants were examined to find out what proportion of lecture material they had retained. It was discovered that, on tests given immediately after the listening experiences, these professional people could recall only about 50 percent of what they had heard. What might the results have been had the tests been given a month, or even a week, later?

If a patient reported to his doctor that he was retaining only half the food that he ate, the alarmed physician would take steps immediately to remedy the situation. Yet if this same person were to admit that he was unable to recall more than half the information passed on to him, nobody would be very much concerned.

If a college student were so physically ill that he

could attend only half his classes, he would probably seek permission to drop the course and ask for a refund of his fees. However, indifferent listening skills could cause the same result—failure to retain fully half the material verbally presented by his teacher. In terms of economics, his impaired comprehension might conservatively be estimated to cost him a thousand dollars or more a year, as well as a sizable segment of life which can never be recaptured.

Four language communication skills are needed by a successfully functioning human: Reading, writing, speaking, and listening. And they are generally taught in this order. But, since all communication is basically oral, and writing—converting sounds to readable symbols that convey meaning—is an artificial device, he who would gain knowledge must first master listening skills.

It has been said: "Listening is the lost l in learning." The emphasis of modern educational procedures is on expression, and, by implication, against listening. Recalling with horror the days when children were "seen and not heard," educationalists have ushered us into a new and wonderful era of feverish, noisy activity geared to our society.

A silent student in a modern classroom obviously has a "personality problem." Everything is done to "draw him out" and to motivate him toward the goal of "self-expression." If he speaks up and contributes, even if he has nothing really valuable to say, all is well.

After many years of teaching, I have reached the conclusion that much "self-expression" is mere undisciplined, unprofitable babble. On the other hand, some researchers have suggested that listening might be the very activity which furthers and expands the knowledge of a person anxious to learn.

A Valuable Educational Tool / 23

Certain information must be acquired only by careful listening. Comprehending the basic ideas and concepts of subjects like music appreciation, speaking skills, and languages is not a natural inherent possession. Written materials may appear to be dull, boring, or uninteresting until we hear them verbalized. Reading a Shakespearean play may cause us to struggle to catch its spirit, but a gifted actor's voice breathes life into the cold print.

We can gain information it would take years of reading to gather, simply by listening. A lecturer may have spent years researching a given field of knowledge, sifting the wheat from the chaff, garnering information from many sources, and consolidating it into a cohesive, logical presentation.

There is a time lag in disseminating printed knowledge. By the time an author has gathered his information, written it down, edited it, and had it appraised and accepted by a publisher, much of the information in his newly-published book is already dated. The lecturer has access to journals, studies, and reports, or even work in progress, and can make this fresh information available to his listeners.

There is interplay between a good speaker and his listeners. If a reader cannot understand the book he is reading, he may just give up. The skillful speaker constantly senses and responds to his listeners' reactions. If he becomes aware that his speaking level is obviously above or below their capacity to comprehend, he can adapt his material to them.

On-the-spot questioning makes immediate clarification possible. In some college classrooms today is equipment which allows the class members to speak directly to an authority in their field of study and ask him questions, providing them the benefit of his most recent thought on the subject.

Listening is also a skill that develops an individual's creativity in an unusual manner. A recent upsurge of interest in a radio program called, "The Radio Mystery Theater" has called attention to the creative aspects of listening. We have come to believe that the visuals of TV are important to the presentation of drama. We must see it. Not so, insists Himan Brown, who has been pushing for the reintroduction of radio theater. The key to what Brown calls the "theater of the mind" lies in developing the art of listening.

After a reaction to, and a swing away from sterile, indoctrinating teaching techniques which allowed no place for pupil participation, educators moved into the activity phase—almost activity for its own sake. Now we must realize physical activity alone is not sufficient. Mental participation, an active listening process, is necessary for meaningful learning.

3
A Resource for Helping Others

A sympathetic listener will frequently provide troubled people an opportunity to better handle emotional pressures. —J.W.D.

The concerns of America's women are nowhere more graphically illustrated than in the tremendous number of beauty shops dotted across the country and dedicated to helping turn out the well-groomed woman. With great regularity milady hurries to her appointment to be primped, prodded, and pampered as she has her hair shampooed, frosted, rinsed, set, or cut; fingernails manicured; toenails pedicured; face worked over; eyebrows shaped; or eyelashes dyed. These attentions apparently help the jaded ego, as is evidenced by the frequently heard statement: "I feel so much better after I have been to the beauty shop."

This unlikely institution may be the new frontier

of psychotherapy, unwittingly demonstrating that beauty is not "only skin deep." Women, spending hours with their operators, pour out stories of trouble with the children, the struggle of money management, thoughtless husbands, and the complexities of a modern woman's life. The intimate details of the most personal aspects of husband-wife relations are enough to make the hair dryer blow a fuse!

And all of this takes place because of the listening ear of a beauty operator!

Sometimes with a limited formal education, but with wide experience of life and senses not too easily shocked, she is well remunerated for her work. Her rate of pay is justified by her possession of unwitting psychotherapeutic skills plus the fact that she need have no professional scruples about accepting a tip. Madam's feeling of well-being as she leaves the salon may in no small measure be related to the operator's capacity to listen.

Some of the reasons people need a listening ear, such as many women find in the beauty parlor, include the four following considerations.

1. *People need to break out of their skin-enclosed isolation.* There is a peculiar sense in which every individual breaks out of his skin-enclosed isolation through speech, beginning the process of establishing word linkages in the world around him. As people listen to the new arrival, they enable him to enter into the community of experience.

Born a normal child, stricken nineteen months later by a mysterious illness, Helen Keller lingered at death's door. Then suddenly and unaccountably she recovered. To her parents' dismay, however, the illness had left Helen deaf and blind; and because of her deafness, she was mute.

Helen became, in her own words, ". . . a Phantom living in a world that was no-world." She described herself as "wild and unruly, giggling and chuckling to express pleasure; kicking, scratching, uttering the choked screams of the deaf-mute to indicate the opposite." She was condemned to stay in this "no-world" for five years.

Then the dedicated teacher, Annie Sullivan, began to work with Helen. At first there was little response. Helen explained, "But alas! Phantom had no sense of 'natural' bonds with humanity."

After a frustrating month, and on the day earlier marked by a ferocious outburst of temper, there finally came the moment of breakthrough. Down at the well, redolent with the smell of honeysuckle, the ever-diligent teacher placed one of the little blind girl's hands under the flowing stream of icy cold water. In Helen's other hand she spelled out the word *water*, again and again, until suddenly "the mystery of language was revealed to me!" Helen recalled. "I knew then that 'w-a-t-e-r' meant the wonderful cool something that was flowing over my hand. . . . That living word awakened my soul, gave it light, hope, joy, set it free."

Words now had significance. Previously Helen had struggled to learn meaningless series of letters; now they combined into words representing something. She learned many words that day, just how many she could never recollect. However, "I do know that *mother, father, sister, teacher*, were among them—words that were to make the world blossom for me 'like Aaron's rod with flowers.'"

These words made "the world blossom" because they were terms of relationship. Because Helen had had no comprehension of experiences of relationship up to this time, it is easy to understand why she had lived in "no-world."

Harry Stack Sullivan says that personality is

"the relatively enduring pattern of recurrent interpersonal situations which characterize a human life." To realize our potential, we must relate to other individuals.

Without someone to give her information, Helen would have remained in "no-world." As a series of people communicated with her—first her teacher; then her family—Helen avidly sought to know the world around her. The imprisoned splendor escaped, and Helen became one of the great creative personalities of her day.

There are many Helen Kellers around us today. They need the all-important listening ear to help them develop their tremendous potentialities and possibilities.

2. *Listening to people helps them apply the test of verbalization to their fantasies.* The test of verbalization is an excellent way to clarify one's thought processes. When a person has a chance to verbalize his thinking, to bring it out in the open, to hear it, and then to see how another responds to it, he often sees the irrationality of his thought processes.

Some psychologists claim one differentiating factor which distinguishes man from other forms of animal life is man's capacity for imagery. This bent for fantasy is a tremendous asset which has helped humans to make great advances.

However, many people have a tendency to withdraw from the realities of life and, by living in an imaginary fantasy world, can easily become confused as to what is fact and what is fantasy. Walter Mitty, in the famous story by Thurber, was dominated by his wife and mother-in-law. By lapsing into fantasy, he saw himself as a great surgeon, a broncobuster, a sea captain, or some other heroic figure, rather than the poor henpecked person he really was.

Many counselors can recall situations in which a

client suddenly stops talking about his problem and says, "No, that isn't the way it really is." In the process of exteriorizing his thoughts for his listener, he has reevaluated them. One man expressed it beautifully: "How can I know what I think, unless I hear myself say it?" Listening to a troubled individual enables him to undertake an evaluation process by applying the test of verbalization.

3. *When we listen we facilitate the process of people's saying something to themselves.* A famous theologian has spoken of man's capacity to talk to himself as "the internal dialogue of self." The need to address oneself is not easily satisfied, but as listeners we can help people accomplish this difficult task.

We might imagine that the easiest way for an individual to speak to himself would be to sit down in a corner and think furiously, but it isn't. Apparently, this task is most easily accomplished by passing on a message to our inner self while speaking to someone else. "Every speaker has two audiences—the people before him in the audience and *himself*," says one psychiatrist.

Psychotherapists have long been aware of this need. At least one school of psychotherapy insists the psychotherapist say little. In a process called *mirroring*, he sits and listens, his responses reflecting the client's statements. The counselor's main function is smoothing the way for the client to say something to himself. When we develop our listening skills, we perform a similar function for those to whom we listen.

4. *Listening helps people to vent the emotions that have built up within them.* The frustrations of life cause emotional intensities to build up rapidly, bringing about a condition of uneasiness. As emotional pressures develop, frustrations build. There

must be some form of release. Like a blocked hose, these emotional pressures cause the personality to erupt in its most vulnerable areas.

A listener who is mature, objective, and permissive enough not to become personally involved or defensive during these emotional outbursts will provide a channel for the draining of the emotion.

Speech has been described as man's most ready safety valve. Counselors have found that when people are allowed to talk about the things that are worrying them, the emotional intensity often subsides. The helping professions abound with words that describe this experience: Marriage counselors call it "ventilation"; psychoanalysts refer to it as "abreaction"; the word *catharsis* is often used by psychologists. In its original use in the Greek drama, *catharsis* literally means "purging of the emotions." Shakespeare apparently understood something of the value of speech as an outlet for emotional pressure, for he wrote:

> Give sorrow words: the grief that does not speak
> Whispers the o'er fraught heart and bids it break.

A significant portion of our constant interaction with the world about us is the receiving and giving of attention. Without receiving attention the individual fails to reach the potentialities of his unfolding personality. If he never gives attention, he will not only fail to gain the knowledge that he needs of the world about him, but he will never develop the capacity to influence other people, never have the peculiar satisfaction that comes from the sense of having exercised such an influence.

When we consider the word *listening* we generally think of a sensory experience—an assimilative communication skill—used to apprehend sounds coming from the world around us. But it is more than a sense on a level with seeing, smelling, touching, and tasting. Listening is also a function that is used to influence other people and a vehicle by which one individual focuses attention on others.

This volume will focus on listening in the common everyday usage of the word—primarily as the experience of giving and receiving attention.

Three Superlatives in Changing Behavior

4
The Greatest of All Gifts

The greatest gift one person can give another is attention. —J.W.D.

What is the most difficult task a man is called upon to perform in his marriage? For my part, I will suggest buying presents for his wife.

Whenever my spouse's birthday or our wedding anniversary draws near, I am conscious of a mounting apprehension. It is certain I was absent when the talent for buying presents was handed out. My reputation is such that when I say to my wife, "I am going to take a couple of hours off to buy you a present," a startled look comes over her face. She says, "Please keep the receipt so I can take it back," or "Please don't; I'd rather do it myself," or "Please don't bother—how much money would you like me to spend?"

It is even more embarrassing when someone

admires one of my wife's possessions and she says, "A birthday present—my wonderful husband gave it to me." I bask in the congratulations of the viewer, then ask her later, "When did I give you *that?*" She smiles and says, "From the money you allowed me two years ago when you didn't buy me a birthday present."

So when I listen to some authority discussing the difficulties of married life and listing in-laws, children, and sex, I want to say: "Forget it; they are all elementary compared with the problems of giving gifts!"

I feel at one with the writer of the ode "Husband's Lament on Mother's Day":

> M is for the mink coat you want, dear
> O is for the opal ring you crave
> T is for the tiny car you'd love, sweet
> H is for the hat that makes you rave
> E is for the earrings you'd admire, love
> R is for the rug on which you'd tread
>   Put them all together they spell BANKRUPT,
>   So I'm giving you this handkerchief instead.

The Nieman-Marcus store has tried to help with this situation. Its lavish Christmas catalog has featured such items as "his" and "hers" airplanes, "his" and "hers" ostriches, a robot, a Chinese junk, a pair of matched camels, each carrying appropriate price tags for the consideration of the well-heeled gift-giver. While the average catalog browser will probably enjoy this insight into the way the "beautiful" people lavish gifts on each other, he is likely to get the idea that he has no chance in the gift-giving stakes. If *you* think this, you are *wrong—wrong—wrong*.

Years of study have convinced me price tags don't show the value of a gift. The greatest gift I can give doesn't cost anything.

"What is the greatest gift a husband can give his wife?" I have asked hundreds of wives this question and have been met with a puzzled silence, seeming to indicate inexperience with such queries. To help my subjects, I volunteer some information. "I can tell you what it *wouldn't* be. It wouldn't be diamonds, a Mercedes, a lake house, a new home, or an around-the-world-trip. It would be none of these things, even though you might think so. In actual fact, you don't want any of these, you want *attention.*"

How Do I Love Thee?

I was delighted to learn, in the course of a conversation with a famous psychologist, that he was interested in the nurture and culture of African violets. It so happened that at this particular time I had developed an interest in these temperamental little flowers and I hoped my learned friend, so skillful in probing the human psyche, might know some secrets about these plants that had caused me so much concern. It turned out that he was a fellow struggler in the horticultural enterprise and had been through many of the same problems as I. As I shared my meager knowledge with my friend, I produced a newspaper clipping setting forth the ten commandments for raising African violets. The last commandment was the clincher. It simply said, "Love them." I looked at my friend and asked: "Love an African violet? What next?"

The outstanding student of human nature smiled and gave me an answer that confirmed his insight as a student of human personality. "Don't you suppose that when it says to love an African violet, it means to look at them regularly, pay a lot of attention to them?"

Once again the psychologist was right, and his comment brought to mind an experience of mine. Because of a speaking engagement it was necessary for me to make a hasty exit from my class and get down the hallway to my office, but my progress was hindered by two students, a male and a female, who were standing in the hallway gazing intently at each other. I was reminded of a snake's mesmerizing a bird.

I pushed my way past this tableau and asked myself, *Why were they looking at each other?* I made a quick decision to return and review the scene. What would cause them to spend so much time gazing at each other?

I looked them over. I couldn't see anything outstanding about *him*. All fellows look about the same to me. I don't know what the girls see in them. Then I focused my attention on *her*. On a scale of 1 to 10, she would have been about 4½. Why this exercise in concentration? Of course, you know the answer—they were in the throes of romantic love.

All of this gives a clue to the nature of love. A psychiatrist has said, "Love is an intense positive interest in an object," and as that loved object becomes aware of all the attention, a feeling of exhilaration follows. *Attention* may be the key to the experiences of love.

P.R. in an Electronics Age

Ronald Reagan's defeat of incumbent President Carter was a tremendous upset. Avowed conservative Reagan's accession to power was viewed with apprehension by many of the liberal-minded citizens of Washington, D.C., and not a few speculated as to the way in which he would be received by the citizens of that city. President-elect Reagan's much-anticipated visit to the nation's capital was headlined in *Newsweek* magazine: "Hail the Conquering Hero." The situation was stated: The President-elect "swept the city's civic and cultural glitterati off their feet simply by paying attention to them."

What an irony that this should have followed the conclusion of a campaign characterized by the most

The Greatest of All Gifts / 39

sophisticated technological techniques, the most highly-developed public relations methods, and the greatest expenditure of money ever lavished on a political campaign! But in developing the most important relationships at the pinnacle of power, the President-elect used the simple but most effective of all techniques, "paying attention."

Many of us have been intrigued and, perhaps, somewhat amused at the stories about Japanese factory workers' wearing uniforms, singing the company song, and doing calisthenics in unison. These activities seem to point to a naïve attitude that readily accepts a regimented approach to life and work. Yet there are other aspects of the Japanese approach that have to do with the relationships within the organization. *Consensus* is the word used to describe the complex process by which many people have a voice in the decisions of the company. The attitude may be summed up in the statement, "Nothing gets done until the people involved agree."

While Americans look on in grudging admiration, many of them nod their heads and murmur, "Remarkable! But it couldn't be done here." Oh, no?

A Sony plant with a glistening white exterior, located in San Diego, is expected this year to manufacture 700,000 color television sets, one-third of Sony's total production. While few of the workers wear the lemon-colored smocks provided by the company, and the characteristic Japanese exercises have been dropped, the emphasis of concern for the workers as members of the company family who are employed for life has continued with remarkable effectiveness. One assembly line worker expressed it, "Working for Sony is like working for your family."

The plant manager—Japanese, of course—insists there are few differences between American and Japanese workers. He points out the main problem is motivating them. The method which he uses with great effect "is to *bathe his U.S. employees in personal attention.*"

The Simple Task That's Not So Simple

The *Newsweek* report about Reagan's "simply paying attention" and the Sony plant manager's strategy of paying personal attention to his employees may need some qualification and elaboration. Like listening, attention—listening's undergirding psychological mechanism—is neither simple nor easy. An examination of the attention phenomenon will quickly show us the reason why few are able to master the skill.

One of the most fascinating sights in our electronic age is a director at work in the control center of a television studio. Despite all that is happening in the studio—the program participants' playing out their parts under blazing lights, and cameramen's maneuvering their cameras for the best shots and superior angles—the real definitive work takes place off the set in the control room. Here the director reigns supreme. Earphones on head, microphone in place, he is conscious not only of instructing the cameramen, lighting specialists, and sound men, but is involved in selecting which of the pictures displayed on at least three monitors will be transmitted over the airwaves or recorded on videotape.

There is a sense in which every individual is a director in his own control room, selecting sensations and impressions that are constantly bombarding us through these multisensory bodies of ours. This selection process is called attention, and we must choose from a number of possible selections.

Once when I presented a program in a small television station, the cameraman demonstrated that he had no artistic pretensions and was set on doing things the easy way. He indicated the spot on which I was to stand, focused the camera on me, checked one more time, and then wandered off, leaving me, in mounting apprehension, trying to make sure I remained in the same spot. Many people feel attention is like that camera, fixed and rigid in its focus—but it is not. It is more appropriate to think of attention as a small child who looks at you for a few moments, then at your hat, then the pattern in the carpet on the floor, then the basket in the corner; then runs to a toy, picks it up, loses interest, and throws it down.

1. *Attention is preeminently mobile.* Attention is a bowl of slippery fish. You reach out and grasp one, only to have it slip through your fingers. Or attention can be a mouse, darting around on the floor exploring its space and finding where it can run. Child, slippery fish, mouse all represent *attention*—which is mobile and exploratory.

One of the most interesting experiences of my life took place on Australia's Great Barrier Reef, where I climbed onto the back of a gigantic sea turtle. The turtle struggled down the beach to the water as I gleefully held on, but once he reached the sea, he shook me off and dived to the depths. I had lost control. Attention is far more mobile than that turtle.

2. *Attention is involuntary.* The basic urges of human personality can be a factor in determining the object to which we give our attention. I once stood in the vestibule of a building with a group of students who were eagerly discussing a theory of personality. In the midst of this animated talk, a very attractive young lady confidently strode past our group, flashing a dazzling smile in our direction. I immediately sensed that I had lost the mobile attention of all the men in the group. A mere male professor had no chance against a pretty girl.

3. *Attention is habitual.* The doctor with his stethoscope hears a murmur completely lost on the untrained ear; the engineer discerns a rumble in the

turbine never heard by the uninitiated; the musician is appalled by a sour note unnoticed by musical illiterates like myself. A man walks into a room and fastens his eye on the framed picture and with a cry of recognition exclaims, "Brass rubbings! Where were they done?" A mother is instantly awakened by her baby's cry. All of these are examples of involuntary attention's functioning because of a mental set or the habits developed over a period of time.

4. *Attention is selective and controllable.* The story is told of the author who was able to write although his small room overlooked the square in which the victims of the French revolutionaries' justice were guillotined. Although the crowd cried for victims, the convicted pleaded for mercy, and the falling blade brought cheers from the bloodthirsty mob, the author's mind was in other places.

If we are to succeed in life, we must learn the exacting task of keeping attention under control. Firefighters find it difficult, as the pressure of water mounts in their hoses, to aim them, as they wriggle, snake, swish, and flop around, often controlling the firefighters rather than vice versa. Maintaining attention calls for more effort than managing fire hoses, because of external as well as internal factors to be overcome.

In a rather clever and apt twist of phrase, a man said of his childhood: "We were so poor, we couldn't afford to pay attention." But, though paying attention costs no money, it is the most expensive gift ever made. The payment comes instead from every effort he can make to withstand the internal personality struggles and the external stimuli which tug him in every direction.

5
A Disease of Epidemic Proportions

The most debilitating social disease is attention deficit disorder. —J.W.D.

Small wonder we Americans are a nation of hypochondriacs. In addition to the constant barrage of TV commercials of an infinite number of medicines for the ills that supposedly afflict us, we have a great number of serious educational and research organizations for fostering interest in diseases and their remedies. The Cancer Society, The Diabetes Association, the Heart Association, The Crippled Children's Society, the Multiple Sclerosis Society, the Muscular Dystrophy Association, and The Reninitis Pigmentosa Foundation all promote worthy causes. I would like to nominate another—The Attention Deficit Disorder Association.

In case this disease is new to you, I would refer you to an imposing volume published by the American Psychiatric Association and referred to by the initiated as DSM-III (Diagnostic and Statistical Manual of Mental Disorders, Third Edition). This most recent formulation of diagnostic categories of mental disorders has set forth a number of new classifications, one of which is *attention deficit disorder.* The category used for children cites "often doesn't seem to listen" as one of the criteria for evaluating this type of reaction. From this perspective, lack of attention *may* be the indication of a mental illness. If we apply this across the boards to adults as well as to children, there are many people who "often don't seem to listen," so may be suffering from this mental illness.

Strangely the judgment of DSM-III of the American Psychiatric Association has been anticipated by that student of human nature, William Shakespeare. This evaluation is seen in the second part of Shakespeare's *King Henry IV.*

The Lord Chief Justice says to Falstaff, "You hear not what I say unto you."

Falstaff replies, "Very well, my Lord, very well . . . it is the disease of not listening, the malady of not marking, that I am troubled withal."

Sufferers from this disorder will obviously be functioning at a less than satisfactory level. Though it might not be the greatest disaster that has ever befallen, a person with this problem might never be able to experience entering a hypnotic trance. Although the Greek root from which our word *hypnosis* comes literally means "sleep", hypnosis is not really sleep. Braid, the Englishman who gave the state of altered consciousness the name *hypnosis,* came to regret his choice. He later stated he would have preferred the word *monoideaism,* because the condition of hypnosis is not one in which the subject is asleep and oblivious to all that is going on round about him.

Rather unfortunately, the practitioners of hypnosis have continued to use the word *sleep* in their induction methods, perhaps because there are few alternatives available. It would be difficult to follow the instructions, "You are going into monoideaism, deeper and deeper monoideaism." There is, in fact, a sense in which the subject, in a hypnotic trance, is more widely awake and more alert than he ever has been before, and the reason for this is his capacity to pay attention.

Attention deficit disorder may also be an indicator of a lowered intelligence level. One of the workshop meetings at a convention of psychologists was conducted by a hypnotist who announced he would put the whole group into a hypnotic trance. Many psychologists are skeptical about the validity of the whole concept of hypnosis. Some of those skeptics in attendance at that meeting overlooked the fact that they were dealing with a hypnotist who was also a psychologist.

The hypnotherapist reminded his audience that research indicates people who are of high intelligence and are willing to cooperate make the best subjects for hypnosis, while people of low intelligence are poor subjects. So, it became a no-win situation for the skeptics. If they maintained their stance, they would be able to debunk the whole concept of hypnosis, but would run the risk of having the true believers label them as low-intelligence subjects. A surprisingly large number of the group of psychologists reported having gone into a trance. The basic concept is that the power to concentrate and pay attention is equated in some ways with intelligence.

Suffering from an attention deficit disorder may affect a person's physical health and strength. Today's great problem of stress is in a large measure related to the primitive "fight or flight" mechanism. This mechanism puts the body's systems into an emergency mode and, in the process, nullifies the body's immune system, allowing it to fall victim to destructive forces.

Dr. Herbert Benson speculates that, in the same way the "fight or flight" mechanism is operative in our bodies, there can also be a countermechanism which releases the immune forces within the body. Benson came up with the idea of relaxation response, induced by these four elements:

1. A quiet environment
2. Concentration on an object
3. A passive attitude
4. A comfortable position.

Easily the most important of these is concentration capacity. The person with an attention deficit disorder will obviously find it difficult, if not impossible, to induce the relaxation response. As improbable as it seems, an individual's health can be affected by his capacity to pay attention.

This book will aim at helping people fight off this dread disease. Every effort will be made to lead you into the pathway of mental health.

6
Cruel and Unusual Punishment

The greatest punishment I can inflict on another person is the withdrawal of attention. —J.W.D.

The eighth amendment of the U.S. Constitution promises citizens they will not be subject to "cruel and unusual punishment." It is highly improbable that most of us will ever experience the traditional ideas of cruel and unusual punishment.

However, in the opinion of some, there is a punishment so cruel and unusual as to be a devastating experience. The Greeks called it "ostracism;" West Pointers refer to it as "silencing;" the British speak of "sending him to Coventry;" POW's were concerned about "solitary confinement;" and those modern behavioral engineers in the psychological field refer to it as "time out."

Since 1972, Robert Bear has been existing in a situation which represents this ultimate punishment. Bear was critical of leaders of the Reformed Mennonite Church and as a result, the church invoked the custom of "shunning." His wife and six children moved out of the house, leaving him to himself. Formerly a prosperous potato farmer, Bear lost his 100-acre property when his wife refused to cosign a loan from the bank. People from the community refused to work for him and he experienced difficulty in selling his produce. Bear has discovered the cruelest punishment the church could inflict on him was to refuse relations with him, and describes his life as "a living hell."

Rather ironically, part of the academic training of professional U.S. Army officers may unwittingly reinforce the use of subtle torture. An example is the exquisite torture to which West Point Cadet James J. Pelosi was subjected.

Pelosi, accused of cheating on an examination, made an impassioned assertion of innocence, and presented conflicting evidence, but the Honor Committee convicted him. However, because of an irregularity in the proceedings, the Superintendent dismissed the verdict.

Despite the Superintendent's decision, the student body decided to punish Pelosi with "silencing." Pelosi ate alone at a table normally occupied by ten, and lived by himself in a room usually housing two or three. The experience took its toll on Pelosi, who lost twenty-six pounds during the seventeen-month period.

On graduation day, the silencing was broken as fellow cadets shook his hand. Pelosi remarked, "It was just as if I were a person again."

Cadet Pelosi said at the conclusion of his West Point period of silencing, "I've taken a psychology course, and I know what isolation does to animals. No one at the Academy asks how it affects a person. Doesn't that seem strange?"

Cruel and Unusual Punishment / 49

Yes, it *is* strange—but psychologists are vividly aware of the effects of isolation. If we wish to decrease certain behavior in a person, one way to do it is to ignore him—to pay him no attention. When the behavior is not rewarded, it will be discontinued in a process psychologists call *extinction.*

Coventry, England, is a great industrial center and the site of two cathedrals—one, in ruins from German bombing during World War II; the other a majestic, modern glass-and-steel structure built as a memorial to British servicemen who lost their lives in the same conflict. It was also the home of Lady Godiva, who put love of her fellow citizens ahead of her natural modesty.

Coventry's chief claim to literary fame, however, lies in the saying, "Send him to Coventry." The saying originated with the king's practice of billeting his soldiers in private homes. The citizens of Coventry had such dislike for this imposition that they refused to have anything to do with these soldiers socially. Any woman seen fraternizing with a soldier was immediately ostracized by her fellow citizens.

Because of this deprivation of all social intercourse, men in the army dreaded an assignment to this city. A dictionary will provide this definition:

send to Coventry: refuse to associate with.

The punishment is devastating because it removes its victim from all possibility of attention.

A cartoon depicted a woman lying on the psychiatrist's couch. To the therapist, sitting with pencil poised above his notebook, the woman is saying, "If only my husband listened to me the way you do." The woman's husband was "sending her to Coventry," perhaps unwittingly, but punishing her just as surely.

If the husband had spent some time listening to her, his marriage might have proved more interesting and more exciting, his wife's emotional adjustment would have been much more satisfactory, and it certainly would have been much cheaper than the psychiatrist's fee of $60 an hour.

Not only is this true of the so-called emotional illnesses, but it may apply to many of the physical maladies that afflict the human frame. In the new approach to illness, sometimes referred to as holistic medicine, it has been discovered the emotional condition of an individual has much to do with his physical well-being, and one of the emotional factors is the amount of attention he gets, or fails to get.

Studies of psychosomatic illnesses emphasize the close interrelatedness of mind and body and lead to the conclusion that sickness is not always what it seems. There are some people who, in the well-known phrase, "enjoy bad health," and have some good reasons, though often unconscious, for not recovering. One of the most significant of these may be that the condition brings attention along with pain.

Most people can see the rationality of this reasoning as it applies to some of the more obvious illnesses as headaches, asthma, or body rashes, but what about such an obviously organic condition as cancer? In one of the most interesting programs in holistic medicine, the patient, diagnosed in a terminal condition, is given a treatment which involves concentration, relaxing, imaging, and group experiences. A question that is asked of the patient in this regimen is, "What is this illness doing *for* you?"

Most patients would be shocked by this question. Their response would be, "Doing *for* me? What is it doing *to* me? It is destroying me, taking my life from me!" Yet, if they will be painfully honest, they will discover sickness does do something for us. It places the patient center stage. His family members, his friends, and his associates then become supporting players as they express their concern. The patient's every wish is given carefully consideration. He is receiving *attention,* in many instances more attention than he has ever received in his life before. His illness is doing much *for* him.

What a tragic situation this turns out to be! Yet many people are apparently willing to pay the high price of cancer, ultimately giving up precious life itself to get attention.

Few professions are considered less dramatic than teaching, but one story of teaching became the basis for a remarkable play and later a highly successful musical. George Bernard Shaw's *Pygmalion,* which blossomed into *My Fair Lady,* is the tale of a speech teacher who, to win a wager with his friend, undertakes teaching a cockney flower girl to speak such flawless English that she could pass for a princess at a great social occasion.

The character of Henry Higgins causes pedagogues to cringe as they observe his teaching technique with Eliza. Domineering, bad-tempered, and sarcastic, he forces his pupil to undertake long hours of monotonous drills while scarcely dropping a morsel of encouragement. Eliza reels under his domineering tutelage, but does not complain, docilely submitting to his soul-deadening regimen.

The moment of triumph comes when Eliza, introduced by Higgins as a Hungarian princess, moves regally among the assembled nobility at the ball, a stunning figure, conversing easily with dignitaries. Her triumph is complete.

Returning home, Eliza, Higgins, and Colonel Pickering gather in the living room to savor their achievement. Pickering and Higgins recall the highlights of the evening and congratulate each other on their accomplishments. Eliza, upon whose achievements alone this success had been achieved, stands to one side, ignored in all their conversation.

Completely devastated, Eliza leaves the Higgins household and heads for Henry's mother's home. Humiliated by Eliza's departure, Higgins begins a frantic search for his protégée. When he finally finds Eliza, Higgins tries to bully her into returning. What had upset her? Why had she left? Had he or Colonel Pickering misbehaved? Had they been cruel to her?

Here was Eliza's opportunity. She could have recounted Higgins' irascibility, his sarcasm, his shouting, his continual drilling until she was ready to drop from weariness. But in these experiences she had been the recipient of his total attention—a possible form of reward.

Eliza's complaint focuses, instead, on Higgins' failure to give her attention. She states it very clearly: "I won't be passed over." This was the greatest punishment Higgins and Pickering could have inflicted upon the flower girl turned princess.

Henry VIII, the king who carried the title "Defender of the Faith," given to him by the Pope before Henry went on to have the English Church sever relationships with the papacy, was also noted for his ambition to father a male child, which would ensure a succession of Tudors to the throne of England. His first wife, Catherine of Aragon, having reached menopause without producing a son who lived to adulthood, was looked upon with disfavor by the petulant monarch and he moved to divorce her. In the process he came ultimately to disavow papal authority.

His second choice for a wife was a vivacious, olive-skinned girl, with black hair that flowed to her waist. Having used many devious means to overcome the numerous obstacles which only seemed to fan the flame of his passion, Henry married her and Anne Boleyn became Queen of England. Once his conquest was made, the amorous Henry's eyes began to wander and within two years he had acquired at least three mistresses.

Anne, who had been spoiled by the monarch's years of adulation, did not realize what was happening. Henry's biographer notes the king made his dissatisfaction with Anne known by his "wounding inattention"—withdrawal of attention.

The behavioral psychologists have made some fascinating applications of the principle of punishing by withdrawing attention. One of the most effective methods of disciplining is to use the technique of T.O. ("time-out"). Time-out simply means that when a child misbehaves he is placed in a totally nonstimulating environment, the bathroom for example, for a specific short period of time, say three minutes. This procedure has been shown to be very effective when carefully applied.

Our problem is that we fail to grasp the principle that attention leads to repetition of behavior while withdrawal of attention causes reduction of behavior. Most of us reverse the situation: We complain about displeasing behavior (pay attention—reward) but when a wife, for example, does something pleasing, we don't say anything (withdrawal of attention—punishment).

Effective listening means rewarding by paying attention—not listening means we punish by inattention.

Listening Levels

Listening Levels

Listening is a multisensory experience by which these sensory impressions are given and received in a variety of ways.

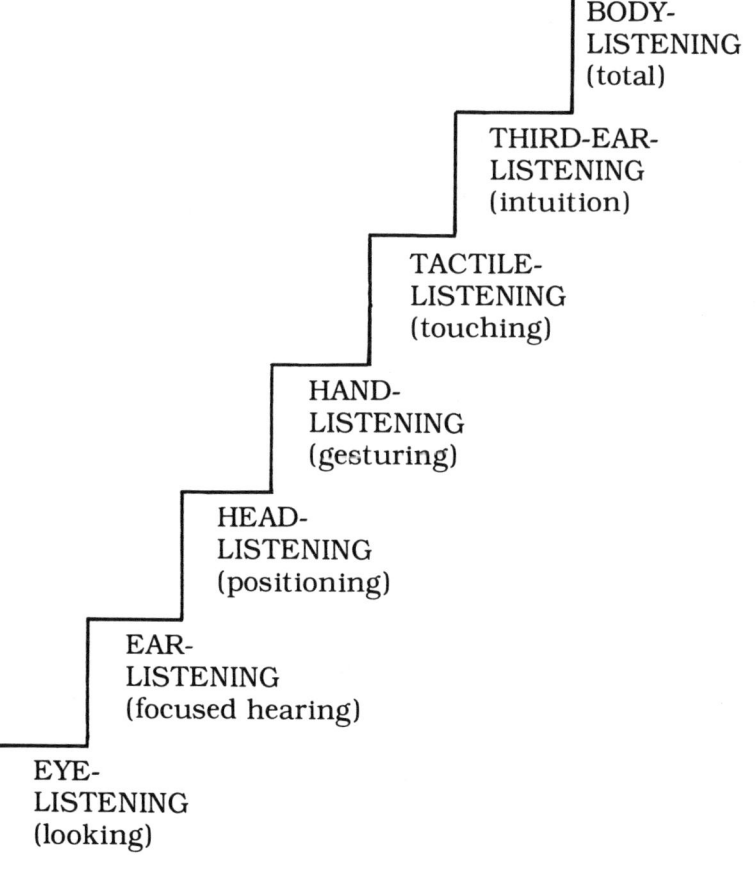

7
Eye-listening

"I pray that the eyes of your heart be enlightened in order that you may know the hope to which he has called you, the riches of his glorious inheritance in the saints" (Eph. 1:18 NIV).

If the dog is man's best animal friend, the honeybee is his best insect friend. The bee cooperates with man, providing some of the most beneficial food humans eat, and playing a highly significant role in strengthening the agricultural enterprise by pollinating the crops. Man has repaid these insect friends by making the honeybee into the most studied of all insects. These studies have shown that among other things the bee has remarkable eyes — so remarkable that their three microscopic lenses have furnished the basic design for glasses for those with minimal sight.

When the bee takes off on its first flight, it circles

the hive *backwards.* It seems as if the bee has within it some mechanism akin to an automatic movie camera, which receives an impression of the total setting of the beehive. This provides the bee with so strong and vivid a built-in map of the hive and its immediate surroundings that, if the hive is moved just a foot or so, the bee may be confused and experience great difficulty in finding its way back home again. What the bee sees is a vital part of its total orientation to life.

Looking Like a Listener

Human eyes are similarly important. In many ways listening begins, not with the ears, but with the eyes. Visual cues are vital to the listening experience.

A listener needs to look the part. A listener who does not look as if he is listening, is for all intents and purposes, no listener at all. Ralph Waldo Emerson stated the situation succinctly—"The eyes of men converse as much as their tongues, with the advantage that the ocular dialect needs no dictionary, but is understood the world over."

Eye-listening is an important part of meeting another person. How is that person dressed—neatly or untidily; expensively or cheaply; modestly or in a showy fashion? What is the general demeanor of this person—confident, tentative, belligerent, deferential? How does he sit—upright, tensely, with both feet on the ground, slouched, with legs crossed? What moods do his eyes convey—furtiveness, apprehensiveness, concentration, sadness?

Nothing is more disconcerting for me than to try to carry on a conversation with someone who is wearing dark glasses. Like the soldiers who were ordered not to fire their weapons until they saw the whites of the enemies' eyes, I feel that if I am going to have a conversation with a person, I need to see the whites of his eyes. On occasion, I say to a client who sits looking at the floor, "Look at me. Let me see your eyes." I want people to listen with their eyes.

The outstanding preacher of the nineteenth century, and perhaps of all time, was the great Britisher, Charles Haddon Spurgeon, often called the "Prince of Preachers." His series of lectures delivered to students in Spurgeon's College were masterpieces of wit and wisdom. In his lecture entitled "Attention!" he points out in his inimitable way that people "attend chapel but don't attend the preacher."

Spurgeon goes on to tell of preaching in a church in which the members of the congregation kept looking around at the great number of latecomers. When the troubled preacher could stand it no longer, he said, "Now, friends, as it is so very disturbing to you to note who comes in, and it disturbs me so very much for you to look around, I will, if you like, describe each one as he comes in, so that you may sit and look at me, and keep up at least a show of decency."

He described a friend whom he could depict without offense as "a very respectable gentleman who had just taken his hat off," and so on. He commented, "After that one attempt I found it was not necessary to describe any more, because they felt shocked at what I was doing, and I assured them that I was much more shocked that they should render it necessary for me to reduce their conduct to such an absurdity. It cured them for the time being, and I hope forever, much to their pastor's joy."

On another occasion he said, "If there is a blind man in my congregation I want him to turn his sightless eyes toward me." Spurgeon wanted his congregation to pay attention with their eyes.

Looking for the Bond of Love

Attention is a significant part of the important experience of "bonding" which establishes a tie between mother and baby immediately following birth. One researcher has attacked the widely-held notion that babies do not see in their early hours of life, and claims newborn babies have shiny, bright, wide-open eyes, capable of focusing and fixing on objects. One pediatrician observed this and commented that the baby's alertness "is especially suited for meeting parents. It often fosters parental feeling and the sense of ecstasy in parents."

The most important aspect of this is *listening with the eyes*—visual attentiveness. Investigators found that when mothers talk to their babies after birth, 80 percent of what they say is related to eyes. A characteristic statement is: "Please open your eyes. If you open your eyes, I'll know you are alive."

Even more striking, most mothers meeting their babies for the first time shift themselves around so that they are face-to-face, with their eyes and the baby's eyes on the same plane of rotation. This action has led to the speculation that mothers are seeking a signal. As one doctor puts it, "a mother can't easily become bonded to her infant unless the baby responds to her in some manner—you can't love a dishrag." All of this give evidence to the poet Yeats' statement, "Love comes in at the eye."

Looking for Mood-Measures

The eyes are the most expressive of our facial features. Their movements, narrowing, widening, their brightness or lack of brightness, all reveal the mood of their owner. And the deliberate *wink* may be the most telling of all eye actions.

Mrs. Harrison, a lady of middle years who has succeeded in remaining youthful despite difficult years on the mission field in a foreign country, specializes, of all things, in the wink—not a flirtatious wink, but a gentle lowering of the top eyelid to join its companion, saying in effect, "You are right—dead right!" This wink is so effective that when she sits in my class during a lecture I find my eye frequently moving in her direction in search of reinforcement. In fact, I find it difficult to resist the urge to reply in the same manner, but I *do* resist, in order to save myself from the accusation that I am carrying on a classroom flirtation with a missionary! Mrs. Harrison is an expert in listening with her eyes.

Looking Toward Survival

Jacobo Timerman tells how he learned to listen with his eyes in the book, *Prisoner Without A Name—Cell Without A Number*. Living in solitary confinement, Timerman was forbidden to look at the world outside the four walls of his cell and the cover on the peephole in his door remained closed almost constantly, opened only occasionally from the outside by a prison guard. When a careless guard left the shutter open, he put his eye to the hole. In the peephole of the door of the cell across the corridor was another eye! Timerman saw the eye begin to blink and he knew that he was not the last human survivor on earth.

Never making a sound or uttering a word, the two prisoners began to play a strange game of visual lost-and-found, moving away from the hole and then returning. This simple incident broke through their isolation and gave a sense of hope to both.

In another example of eye-listening, a military intelligence man was able to receive the message an American prisoner of war was trying to get back to his fellow countrymen. During the Vietnam conflict Jeremiah Denton, Jr., now the U.S. Senator from Alabama, was one of the P.O.W.'s interviewed by North Vietnamese in a propaganda film. Denton and the others stated they were being treated in accord with the requirements of the Geneva Convention. But the alert intelligence man, viewing the film, noted the way Denton was blinking. Did his eye movement result from prison diet and treatment, or could it mean something else?

They ran and reran the film, carefully scrutinizing the blinks and finally concluding they were a way of sending a message in Morse code. One long blink was "T"; three long closures, "O"; then the short-long-short pattern of "R"; another long closure, "T"; two short blinks and a long one, "U"; short-long-short again, "R"; and then a quick blink, "E". The word *torture* was read by the man who was listening with his eyes.

Had Denton not known Morse code, he would have lost the one viable option of communication open to him as a prisoner of war. But his knowledge would have been in vain had there not been someone who was able to *listen with his eyes.*

Some professionals are not enthusiastic about the use of the term *lip reading.* They point out that the so-called lip reader receives a number of visual cues, along with the speaker's lip movements. The principle of "visual listening" applies to people who may have the most acute hearing: To get the message, one must listen not with his ears alone, but visually as well.

We must learn to use our eyes—really use them, if we are to hear with our hearts. Looking around the room, cataloging the books on the shelves, or staring into space is not the way to give a person our best gift—our attention. Looking at that person carefully, so carefully—giving the subject our gentle, interested, concerned gaze—assures him that we intend, not to pry, but to help.

Visual Listening

Here is an exercise in listening with the eyes. This "Message from Earth" was inscribed on a 6" x 9" aluminum plate, anodized with erosion-resistant gold and attached to the space vehicle Pioneer X in the hope that it might reach dwellers in space.

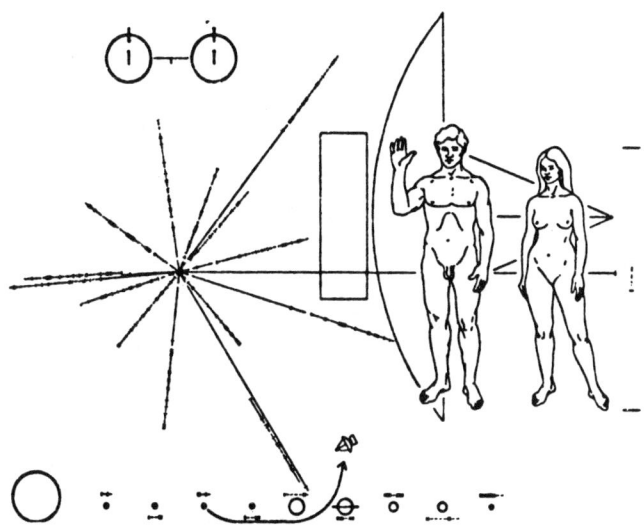

But what is the message?

In a test, a copy of this plaque was shown to over 100 people, all college graduates, some with doctor's degrees. Not one of them was able to decipher the message.

It would be easy to speculate that the residents of another planet who rushed over to pick up the remains of Pioneer X would see the plate and excitedly take it to their scientific authorities. These learned individuals might well conclude that earthlings were nudists—the men, muscle-bound weight lifter types and the women, dumpy little gals with long straight hair—who probably communicated with one another by means of strange geometric designs, circles, and dots.

Following is the official interpretation of the plaque's inscription. Read it through.

The radiating lines at left represent the positions of fourteen pulsars—cosmic sources of radio energy—arranged to indicate our sun as the home star of the launching civilization. The "1—" symbols at the ends of the lines are binary numbers that represent the frequencies of these pulsars at the time of the launch of Pioneer X relative to that of the hydrogen atom shown at the upper left with a "1" unity symbol. The hydrogen atom is thus used as a "universal clock," and the regular decrease in the frequencies of the pulsars will enable another civilization to determine the time that has elapsed since Pioneer X was launched. The hydrogen atom is also used as a "universal yardstick" for sizing the human figures and outline of the spacecraft shown on the right. The hydrogen wavelength—about eight inches—multiplied by the binary number representing "8" shown next to the woman give her height—sixty-four inches. The figures represent the type of creature that created Pioneer. The man's hand is raised in a gesture of good will. Across the bottom are the planets, ranging outward from the sun, with the spacecraft's trajectory arcing away from the earth, passing Mars, and swinging by Jupiter.

8
Ear-listening

"Let your ear be attentive" (Neh. 1:6 NIV).

In his book *Witness*, Whittaker Chambers relates an experience which led him to abandon his atheism and ultimately his membership in the Communist party. As he stood one day, looking down at his daughter, he was overwhelmed by the beautifully intricate formation of her ear. He finally concluded, "No, those ears were not created by any chance . . ."

Any inquirer who pauses to consider the subject of human auscultation—the act of listening—must not only be impressed by the shape of the ear, but by complex human audition as well.

The Wonder of Hearing

The mechanism of the ear is made up of three parts: The external ear, the middle ear, and the inner ear. All play a peculiar role in the hearing process.

The *outer ear* includes the delicately sculptured and arranged auricle, a sound trumpet which catches the sound waves and guides them into the auditory channel, a passage of about one-and-a-half inches, the outer third of which is lined with tiny, wax-producing glands, and fine hairs that constitute a gentle but effective barrier to inquisitive insects and foreign bodies.

Separating the outer ear from the *middle ear* is the eardrum, or tympanic membrane, a thin sheet of tissue about a quarter of an inch in diameter. Sound waves cause the eardrum to vibrate, touching the first of three closely linked moveable bones. The unusual shapes of these bones have given them their picturesque names. Attached to the eardrum is the malleus or hammer, which rests against the incus or anvil that in turn impinges on the stapes or stirrup.

Sound vibrations move the stapes or stirrup in and out of an oval window in the cochlea, a snail-shaped mechanism also known as the *inner ear,* causing some of the 24,000 fibers of the basilar membrane to vibrate and stimulating the attached nerves.

The neural current then flows through the auditory nerve to the temporal lobe of the brain, which provides a fantastic number of circuits that can be hooked up in a great variety of directions.

Assaults on Our Ears

There may be some plain, ordinary physical reasons for children's notorious inability to hear what their parents are saying! The noise pollution of modern life may easily have taken its toll on their delicate hearing systems and associated listening activities. Otologists, specialists in hearing problems, report that years of electronically amplified rock-'n'-roll music which researchers point out may reach as high as 125 decibels, may result in early hearing loss.

During the trip home from a dance, an interested medical man noticed that his teen-aged daughter wasn't hearing what he was saying. His curiosity aroused, the doctor paid a visit to the next dance and set up some monitoring equipment, which revealed that the band's sound level peaked at 120 decibels. Following the conclusion of the dance, further tests indicated that, despite their youthful resilience, the kids showed an average hearing loss of eleven decibels, and one boy showed a thirty-five decibel loss.

So when Junior, in response to the question: "Why didn't you do what I told you?" responds: "I didn't hear you," there's a chance he may be honestly reporting the results of years of exposure to ear-splitting rock-'n'-roll music.

This phenomenon is not confined to children and young people. Mary Telfer is increasingly frustrated at her spouse's lack of response to many of her choicest statements. *He just ignores me,* she sometimes thinks. But his apparent lack of attention could possibly be related to his military service.

When a man joins the U.S. Army, one of the grave dangers he faces, despite excellent medical services, is loss of hearing. Army authorities report this to be the number-one occupational health hazard for all combat troops, affecting approximately 30 to 50 percent of all active duty Army personnel. For some, the effects are temporary; for others, the loss is permanent. The Veterans Administration estimates that it pays more than fifty million dollars annually in compensation for service-connected hearing losses.

The soldier's leisure hours as well may confront him with this hazard. Entertainment provided for the troops in recreation centers often includes loud music. Damage to hearing from this source has already been proven. One sensible suggestion that has been made is to attach electronic sensors or squelch devices on sound equipment used in many service clubs, to turn on warning lights, or shut down the sound emitter if the noise exceeds the limits of safety.

The small plastic container attached to the soldier's jacket is not intended to embellish the uniform. It encloses ear plugs, and indicates the Army's concern for his hearing.

Despite all these precautions, the social conversation of a group of artillery officers has been described by one officer's wife as a shouting match. The potential difficulties between people whose ears may have suffered in this way are readily recognized.

These assaults on the ears create all sorts of obstacles to an ear-listening experience. As we will later see, the would-be listener may have to redouble his efforts to compensate for the damage to his audio equipment.

Just One Thing After Another

Communication itself is a chain of events—a step-by-step process. Understanding the steps gives us some clues as to where communication goes astray.

The case of Helen White provides a starting point. Helen tells her husband, Bruce, that she feels the housekeeping budget should be increased. She reinforces her case with an information source—the reports of friends' housekeeping budgets and the amount of money Bruce saves for his biannual hunting trips. Helen proceeds to *encode* her message—she takes great care in choosing the words she uses to discuss this touchy subject. Bruce frequently complains that Helen speaks too softly, so she *transmits* her message by raising the volume of her voice. The message moves along the *channel*, traveling from Helen's mouth to Bruce's ears.

As the *receiver,* Bruce looks straight at Helen so he can both see and hear her in order to understand the message. Bruce is busily engaged in *decoding*—trying to make sure he understands what Helen means as she sprinkles her statements with such expressions as "sky-high prices," "staples," and "mad money." The message arrives at its *destination*—Bruce's brain. He evaluates Helen's proposition and weighs the pros and cons of increasing the housekeeping allowance.

Though this may sound fairly simple, it is actually an oversimplification of an infinitely complex operation which, like all complex procedures, can easily get out of gear. The main problem comes from the nature of the communication experience. Because it is a chain of events, it is possible for communication to break down at any one or more of the links. Beginning in one brain and following in sequence until the destination of another brain is reached, the process can easily be disrupted at a number of sensitive *distortion points.* Because a chain is only as strong as its weakest link, each of these points is of equal significance.

Seven possible distortion points can be seen in this incident:

- As Helen thinks about her situation, she may have some wrong ideas—Type A Distortion.
- When she verbalizes her thoughts, she may choose the wrong words—Type B Distortion.
- As she speaks, she could make an emphasis that would change the meaning—Type C Distortion.
- The children may be making a noise that will interfere with the message as it passes from Helen's lips to Bruce's ears—Type D Distortion.
- Bruce's imperfect hearing may cause misunderstanding—Type E Distortion.

- Bruce may be puzzled over some of his wife's expressions, like "mad money"—Type F Distortion.
- The proposition or the message may become complicated—Type G Distortion.

This brief description illustrates the complexity of people-to-people communication. Merely saying that two people have a communication problem is a gross oversimplification.

The most prestigious of all athletic events is the marathon, a foot race exactly twenty-six miles, 385 yards in length. The race has its origin in Greek history. In 490 B.C., the young Greek, Pheidippides, ran from Marathon to Athens, a distance of twenty-six miles, 385 yards, to carry the news of Grecian victory over the Persians, only to die of exhaustion after shouting the joyous tidings: "Rejoice, we conquer!"

Like Pheidippides, the message transmitted by one individual may successfully run a long and hazardous route, only to collapse at its ultimate destination—the ears of the other individual.

Ear-listening demands that one listen in a special way, considering the possibilities of distortion. To be effective, the listener must ask himself some of the following questions:

- Do I understand the basic idea the person is trying to communicate to me?
- Is vocabulary a problem? Does he use words that are unfamiliar to me? What do these words really mean to him? An interruption to ask, "Please explain what you mean" doesn't necessarily offend, but may be seen as an indication of special interest.
- How does he/she express himself/herself? Does an accent, a speech defect, a monotone delivery, or speaking too softly or too loudly cause me to tune the speaker out?

- Do noises on the channel cause me to try to cope with the interference, thereby missing the message?
- Do I feel that everybody is mumbling? This could be an indication of the need to have my hearing tested.
- Do I put forth the effort to understand the concept or idea being expressed and give it my intellectual attention?

Ear-listening would seem to be the most obvious of all types of listening. Unfortunately, the malfunction of a person's basic physiological equipment, along with the chain of events that constitutes a listening experience, provides seven distortion points which may prevent our receiving a message from another person.

9
Head-listening

"Lift up your heads, . . . that the King of glory may come in" (Ps. 24:7 NIV).

A man once spoke about his preacher, an earnest man who didn't always get as much encouragement in his preaching as he needed from his rural congregation. Said this sensible man, "I've found a way to help my preacher. If I sense he needs encouragement —and I'm sorry to say he often does—I begin to nod my head. You should see him respond! I feel my head is like the handle on a pump; the more I move it, the more he spouts." The preacher was responding to a listening head.

We need to listen with our heads! Sitting like a bump on a log, or looking like a propped-up cadaver will provide little motivation for a speaker.

But nodding can also be a deterrent to clear communication. In the years of the Turkish occupation of Macedonia, the conquerors organized a massive effort to convert the native Yugoslavs to the Muslim faith. Apprehending a native, they would place a scimitar at his throat and ask, "Do you believe in Muhammad?"

The subject, vividly aware of his situation, would vigorously nod his head backward and forward in the universally accepted gesture to indicate yes. The response satisfied both parties, because the wily Yugoslavs had agreed among themselves to reverse meanings. For them, turning the head sideways from left to right indicated yes, while nodding backward and forward indicated no.

Head in Hand

Said to be the greatest sculptor of his day, the French artist Auguste Rodin was more concerned with realistic art than beautiful art. One of his most famous sculptures is "The Thinker."

"The Thinker" indicates by the position of his head his readiness to grapple with any new idea that comes his way. He rests his head, burdened with heavy thoughts, upon his fist.

Listening critically can also be indicated by an individual's putting his head in his hand, but with his forefinger resting against the side of his face. One experienced public speaker tells of looking over his audience as he addresses it, judging its receptiveness by the number of auditors who sit with their heads in this position. These are the critics, whose listening habits may be compared to the feeding habits of a flock of seagulls. They wait for some morsel of food or knowledge to be tossed into the air, then snap it up, fussing about the quality of the offering.

The distinctive position in which the subject leans back in a chair with the back of his head resting on locked fingers has come to be seen as a listening position of relaxed readiness.

Investigators have turned up many drawings of frontiersmen sitting with pistols on hips, hands laced behind their heads. Of latter days, some observers have noted this gesture being used by attorneys as they give attention to a client as he pours out his story.

But perhaps one of the worst types of head-in-hand-listening is head-in-palm, accented with drooping eyes, eyelids half-descended. This position gives the impression that if the listener's hand were not supporting his head it would certainly roll forward. His message is: "Poor me! I've got to put up with this, but please hurry up and get it over."

Angle As an Indicator

Some studies have shown that the angle at which a person's head is held is another indicator of how much attention is being paid.

As an audience sits in a group, like the sunflowers turning toward the sun, the movement of heads toward the tilted position is a frequent indication of a developing interest—a good listening attitude.

But a head held in a rigid upright position position may have another meaning as a listening technique. Soviet dictator Josef Stalin's biographer, Deutscher, suggests Stalin had a unique gift and was unsurpassed in the art of patient listening. With head held perfectly still, except for the movement of his lips as he pulled on his pipe, Stalin listened *immovably*. Later, after the midnight knock at the door, the secret trial, and the journey to the forced labor camp, the memory of that immobile head may have come back to haunt the victim.

Head-listening is varied by a process of lifting the head and stroking the chin or beard. In *Fiddler on the Roof*, Tevye engages in this activity as an indication of reflective listening, as he takes his concern to a high level, calling on the Almighty to offer some explanations of his behavior. The attitude of stroking the chin is generally seen as a process of evaluation—"let me see. . . ."

One Good Listener

Dr. Ralph D. Nichols of the University of Minnesota once addressed a high-school commencement in which, from his point of view, everything went wrong. One child began to cry; then another swelled the chorus. A small boy galloped up and down the aisle, chased by another. With the sinking feeling only a public speaker knows, Nichols realized he had lost his audience.

Nichols tried every trick of the speaker's trade. He spoke more loudly, told a funny story, walked around the stage, peered intently and disapprovingly at the area of disturbance. But all was to no avail.

Then he tried his last desperate trick. He found one good listener—an elderly gentleman in the first row who was looking up, smiling, and nodding his head approvingly. Concentrating all his attention on this one listener, the speaker gradually salvaged the situation and the speech.

During the refreshment period that followed, Nichols asked the school superintendent to introduce him to the old gentleman who had sat on the front row.

"Well, . . . I'll try to introduce you," said the superintendent, "but it may be a little difficult. You see, the poor old fellow is stone-deaf."

Unable to listen with his ears, the deaf man had saved the day by listening with his head.

The Art of Head-listening

Head-listening is quite an art. Common usage may have given us a wrong perspective. My mother, a dedicated churchgoer, had a tendency to close her eyes during the sermon. When I accused her of sleeping, she was quick to point out that she merely closed her eyes so she could better concentrate on the message. I replied, "That may be so, but why do you nod at the same time?"

The association of nodding and sleep was given an impulse by the author Swift, when he referred to a mythical land of sleep called "Nod." For the children of an earlier time it became a part of nursery talk to refer to a nap as entering "the land of Nod."

All of this talk has done a grave disservice to the noble art of nodding. Nodding can be more than an indicator of sleep. It can be the epitome of attention, performed with the finesse of a ballet dancer. The direction of the nod, the speed, and the accompanying movement of nose, eyes, and mouth all convey a message of the listener's interest.

10
Hand-listening

"Clap your hands, . . . shout to God with cries of joy" (Ps. 47:1 NIV).

One of the most exhilarating experiences of theater I've ever witnessed was a one-man performance which held the audience spellbound for nearly three hours. The material presented was a complete book of the Bible, the King James Version of the Gospel of Mark—in Elizabethan English!

An outstanding feature of the presentation was the actor's use of gestures, particularly the movements of his hands. When he came to the portion of the Gospel in which Jesus said, "Suffer the little children to come unto me" (Mark 10:14), he leaned over from his seated position and stretched out his hand in a gesture of invitation.

Sitting near the front of the auditorium was a little girl, whom I had earlier concluded would be bored stiff before the evening was over. However, during the entire performance, the child had followed the actor with wide eyes. As the thespian made his gesture of invitation, she rose from her seat and walked to the edge of the platform. The gesture had been a compelling summons the little girl could not resist.

Negative reactions can be transmitted by hand gestures as well.

My small son once decided he would like to see the countryside and traveled with me on a week's lecture circuit. I enjoyed giving the same lecture each evening, becoming more verbose with each passing day. He, on the other hand, discovering the old adage that "familiarity breeds contempt," became increasingly bored with the whole thing.

The final lecture of the circuit took place in a small country town, in a stifling atmosphere and before a sparse audience. Not the finest moment of my lecturing career, the audience and my utterance were less than inspired.

Then I was perplexed to see my son making strange gestures in the air as I struggled on with my presentation.

After our departure from the meeting place, I questioned my son: "Whatever on earth were you doing while I was speaking?"

He repeated his gesture, adding, "I was writing the word *stop* in the air!"

Messages from Motions

The flying fingers of an interpreter to the deaf help us to realize how aptly gestures can turn verbal statements into nonverbal messages. Not so obvious is the fact that messages are conveyed by a complex but informally organized system of gestures, which can be used as a means of commendation that can help reinforce behavior.

Mr. Dalton doesn't get to the P.T.A. meetings very often, though his wife tries to encourage him in every way she can. She is president this year, and Mr. Dalton made a special effort to be at her first meeting but arrived about ten minutes late. As he took his seat, he looked over at his wife who held her circled finger in a gesture that obviously said, "Thanks, Honey, I knew you'd make it."

Of course, if Mrs. Dalton were in Brazil, the circled finger gesture would have taken on some unsavory associations. The appropriate gesture of approval there would be closing the fingers of the hand with thumb in an upright position. Strangely enough, *this* gesture of approval has a different connotation in some other countries. All of which reminds us that the meanings of gestures are determined by both context and culture.

The sight of people clapping their hands is so sweet to a performer that the Italian opera houses actually employ *claques*—professionals who applaud the performances. When a Russian is applauded, he will join in the applause himself.

Though the opinion of lawbreakers has never counted much with me, the standing ovation given me by a group of inmates in a penitentiary gave me a sense of well-being that has seldom been excelled on any other occasion.

. . . Louder Than Words

The greeting customs of many people give mute evidence of the truthfulness of the saying that actions speak louder than words. A Hungarian friend, though a humble and kind person, greets me with such a clicking of heels that I feel an appropriate response would be to return a military salute. His greeting contrasts with that of an Indian who makes me feel as if I have been deified as he obsequiously puts his palms together and bows his head.

The Russian bear hug may represent the Marxian dialectic of warmth and warning. Anglo-Saxon handshakes range from the enthusiastic bone-cruncher to the "dead fish" dropped into the greeter's waiting hand.

The Beauty of Gestures

In the great evangelical revival of eighteenth-century England, three outstanding personalities emerged. Charles Wesley was the golden voice, wrote over 6000 hymns, and was instrumental in teaching the British people to sing religious songs. John Wesley was an excellent organizer-administrator whose plans were matchless. George Whitefield was the preacher who impressed Garrick the actor to proclaim that the preacher could pronounce the word *Mesopotamia* in such a way as to move an audience to tears.

The fastidious Lord Chesterfield once heard Whitefield describe a blind beggar struggling to keep his balance on the edge of a precipice. When the preacher gave a deft twist of his outstretched hand, Chesterfield jumped to his feet and cried out, "Good God! He's gone!" The gesture had told its own dramatic story.

During a visit to Germany, my discussion with a chaplain's wife indicated she was working with children. In reply to my question concerning the age group with which she was working, the lady held up her hand, thumb and little finger touching, with the remaining fingers indicating the age of three. It was done with exactly the same gesture with which I have seen three-year-old children respond when asked their age.

Through transactions at the commodities market in Chicago, the largest in the world, millions of bushels of wheat, corn, oats, rye, and soybeans are bought and sold—some of which have not yet been harvested, or even planted. The transactions for these 5000-bushel lots are carried out by hand signals. An observer describes the scene, ". . . palm up and in when the broker is buying and up and out when he is selling. Fingers are held horizontally and manipulated to indicate prices offered or asked." Intricate negotiations involving great quantities of produce and large sums of money are expertly carried on without words.

A man can convey an unspoken message by the way he straightens his tie, toys with his glasses, adjusts his belt, or bites his fingernails.

I once sat with a counselor as a woman poured out a sordid story. The counselor listened and uttered never a word as she recounted her experiences. At last she paused, then asked, "What do you think of that?"

The counselor looked at her for a moment, then held his nose between two fingers. That gesture spoke more eloquently than any words he could have spoken.

11
Tactile-listening

"And the people all tried to touch him, because power was coming from him and healing them all"
(Luke 6:19 NIV).

The skin is the largest organ of the body, with an average surface spread of more than eighteen square feet and containing five million sensory cells. When an infant is born, his primary experience of the world around him comes through touching. His first understanding of others is through his skin, and without the sensitive cells in his lips, he would never know the very source of life. This realization has led many experts in obstetrics to try to encourage as much contact as possible between mother and baby.

Some experiments at the University of Colorado Medical Center have shown what happens when infant monkeys were denied contact with their mothers. After the baby monkeys were separated from their mothers, they began to display a variety of distressed behaviors. They stood hunched in the corner of their cage, looking sad, helpless, and confused. They continually sought to touch the other monkeys. Tiny radios linked to sensors on the baby monkeys' bodies proved that their body temperatures, heart rates, and brain wave patterns were altered and their immune systems, disturbed.

After ten days the babies were reunited with their mothers. Following three or four days of continuous holding by their mothers, the distressed babies began to return to more normal behavior. The observers concluded the loss and restoration of the mothers' touch was a significant factor in the functioning of the baby monkeys.

A Misunderstood Method

Touching may be the most misunderstood method of paying attention. In our society we associate touching with sexual overtures—touching the wrong people for the wrong reasons. Therefore, many people are astonished to see a group of burly football players gather around to commend, by touching, a team member who has made a good play.

Some years ago a school principal from Australia visited our home. She was referred to as the "headmistress" and her capability and dignity gave her a certain aura of untouchability. During her visit to my Texas home, she had been her charming, yet slightly aloof self. After politely shaking hands in farewell, I impulsively put my arms around her and gave her a hug. She snuggled in. In a letter she thanked me, in her Australian style, "for that beaut hug."

The Needed Touch

There are many people in our society who need touching—children and the elderly particularly.

A clinical psychologist who worked at one time in the heart unit of a hospital tells of an experience made more poignant because the principals in the story were his parents. The seventy-five-year-old father was nearing death, and knew it. His one simple request was that his wife of nearly forty-eight years should stay by his bedside. The writer describes his mother as his father's life ebbed away: "She gently stroked his hand for hours as his body temperature slowly dropped, until late in the evening he died peacefully, ending a lifteime of exquisite dialogue." At this climactic moment when her husband could no longer speak with his mouth, his wife listened with her hands.

A visitor to a Continental orphanage noted a large peasant woman carrying a baby on her hip and was told, "That's old Anna. Whenever a baby gets sickly for no apparent physical reason, Anna takes it, carries it around, holding it close to her body and giving it bodily contact and affection." It has long been known that the loss of bodily contact may have injurious effects on children.

Children need many such experiences of touch. Whenever a father asked his little girl what story she wanted to hear, she made the same request. Becoming rather bored with the routine telling of the story, daddy recorded it and showed the little girl how to operate the cassete player. Shortly afterward she came to him, again requesting "the story." Daddy responded, "But you have it on tape." The little girl replied, "Yes, I know, but the cassette player doesn't have a lap."

The Laying on of Hands

Experiences can be meaningful to adults as well. The seventy citizens of Juffure, a village in Gambia, West Africa, gathered in a circle around the *griot* (storyteller), who was the repository of the clan's oral history. With these people stood Alex Haley, the writer of the widely-acclaimed book, *Roots*, listening as the griot recited the genealogy of the tribe. Then he came to a dramatic event: "Kunta went away to chop wood and was never seen again."

Haley's excitement mounted as he recalled hearing his grandmother on the front porch in Henning, Tennessee, tell about an ancestor, "the African whose name was Kunta Kinte, who was enslaved and forceably transported to America." Haley showed his notebook record of the incident to the interpreter, who passed on the information to the villagers.

The Binding Touch

As they listened the villagers grew agitated, spontaneously rose to their feet, and began to move in a counterclockwise circle around Haley. As they moved, chanting, a woman pushed her baby into his arms and retrieved it, then another, and another, each thrusting a baby into his arms, then taking it back. It was the ancient ceremony of laying on of hands, and it meant, "Through this flesh which is us, we are you and you are us."

The Healing Touch

While serving as chaplain of a large army hospital I had occasion to accompany a fine dermatologist of Polish origin and training on his rounds. When we stopped before a bad case of dermatitis, the nurse removed the dressings to show the badly infected skin. Without a moment's hesitation the dedicated doctor leaned over and began to rub his fingers over the infected spots. The onlookers as well as the patient were amazed. Smiling into the patient's face, the dermatologist assured him that everything was going to be all right.

Back in his office later, the doctor explained to me that, in his medical training, he had been taught never to show fear in the presence of infection. "A confident attitude helps to quell the apprehensions of the patients," he said. But it *could* be that the contact of the doctor's hands helps to break down the isolation which sickness sometimes brings.

The Lifting Touch

Touching may have unusual by-products. In an experiment, the check-out clerks at the library of an American university were told to conduct their procedures in a standardized fashion. But they were further instructed to touch every other person as fleetingly and insignificantly as possible when handing back his identity card.

As he left the library, each borrower was questioned. The borrowers who went through the normal procedures were unimpressed with what had happened to them. But the ones who were touched, though often failing to remember the *touch*, referred to the smiling librarian or felt their mood elevated after checking out the books. The touch had a potential for changing the person's attitude.

The Affirming Touch

Once in my clinical experience, I was trying to conduct group therapy in a prison hospital, in an experiment with convicted drug addicts. I found, through many futile and frustrating sessions, that these men were real experts at "conning" people. Then came a breakthrough, in a remarkable session of openness and confession. Following the session, the chaplain, who had been present in all the group meetings, excitedly shook my hand saying, "They really accepted you today."

"How do you know?" I asked.

"Didn't you see the way they came around and touched you?"

I was vividly aware that instead of just wandering away after the meeting, the men had congregated about me, hugging, touching, and shaking hands. Their touch was the indication they were really listening to me.

A New Movement

I suppose it had to come sometime, but when it happened, it took me by surprise. We have all heard about alcoholics, and then there were *foodaholics* and *workaholics*. Now there are "hugaholics." The originators of this concept are Charles and Ann Faraone, who have noticed that, in the crisis moments of life, people need someone to open arms wide and embrace them. Unfortunately our society has placed taboos on the practice of hugging, centering around the idea that any bodily contact inexorably leads to a sexual encounter. While the embrace leading to sex has been widely popularized by the media, the non-sexual hug has been downgraded and the would-be huggers, intimidated. So the Faraones have launched a newsletter, "Let's Hug," and prepared a unique greeting card which is a hug coupon, saying, "Good for one hug, redeemable from any participating human being." Hugaholics may be pioneering a new and significant era in human relationships.

Learning to Touch, Touching to Learn

A report has come of a medical student who is learning anatomy by listening with his hands. John Hartman, a student in Temple University's School of Medicine, has developed a new method of studying anatomy by touch, plunging his hands into the cadaver and learning the shape, location, and distinctive feeling of bones and organs by handling them. John is the first blind student of this century to be accepted by a medical school. At last report he was in the top quarter of his class.

In much the same way as this medical student is educated through the use of touch, we are learning that developmental processes in human personality are facilitated or impeded by the presence or absence of touch.

Let us learn to listen with our hands. People need physical contact—a touch which can convey messages that cannot be expressed in words. And it is the unlovely who particularly need our touch—not the voluptuous girls and handsome men who probably get more than they need in any case. Remember the leper: "Jesus . . . touched him" (Matt. 8:3).

12
Third-ear-listening

"The ear of the wise seeketh knowledge"
(Prov. 18:15).

*L*istening with the Third Ear, by the celebrated psychoanalyst Theodor Reik, was one of the most influential books in the early days of the psychotherapy movement. The title carried a message, indicative of the way in which the counselor must listen for the unspoken message contained in the emotional overtones of the speaker's voice.

The counselor's skill is no more evident than in the exercise of third-ear-listening. One counselor reported the case of the woman who said, "I hate my husband." The counselor commented, "The very intensity with which she made the statement indicated that she loved him very much." Taking the woman's statement literally could have had some very important effects on the outcome.

Divising listening tests has been a continuing, difficult task. One well-known test consists of a statement made by a professional, followed by four possible meanings for that statement. The listener's skill is shown by his choice of the message conveyed. Discussion of the test reveals that the listener's cues include the general tone of the speaker, changes in the pitch or tone of the voice, the quality and clarity of the voice, the emphasis placed on a particular word or group of words. Discovering this involves a process that has been called "listening beyond the words."

What Did You Really Say?

My introduction to American academic life was immeasurably complicated by a communication problem. I had just arrived in America from Australia to commence my studies and was somewhat apprehensive. My first night was spent alone in a dormitory room, because the student with whom I was to share it was a "no-show." The night was hot; the building, not air-conditioned. I tossed and turned on a strange bed in anticipation of the arrival of a roommate about whom I periodically indulged in some mental speculation.

The following morning I went to the communal bathroom, and as I entered, saw a fellow student standing there shaving. He turned, looked at me, and addressed me with a strange question: "What do you say?"

I pondered this for a moment, then tried to get some clarification. I responded in my best Australian manner, "I beg your pardon."

My erstwhile friend looked a little startled, then repeated, "What do you say?"

Compelled to reconsider the subject, I changed my approach. "Excuse me, I didn't say anything."

The man looked more than a little startled,

perhaps even shocked; then he muttered something like, "Skip it."

Returning to my room, I reviewed the incident. What was going on in this situation?

The student, upon seeing a person enter the room, had sent me a message. He was saying, in effect, "I'm a human being; you are a human being. You look lonely. I'm going to reach out to you. 'What do you say?'"

My problem was that I wasn't listening with my third ear. I was absorbed in the literal content of his words.

Emotional vs. Intellectual Listening

Jerry Kramer, an offensive lineman for the invincible 1967 Green Bay Packers, developed a technique for preparing himself for each game. He would conjure up a mental image of the man he would be facing. Then he spent the week prior to the game getting into a combative frame of mind by actively hating his opponent. When the Packers were playing the San Francisco Forty-niners, Kramer knew the man to hate was a six-foot, four-inch, 270-pound Texan named Charlie Krueger. Kramer worked at it all the week, thinking of Krueger as the most hateful, contemptible scum of the earth, and building a combative attitude toward him.

Kramer had discovered from experience that he could not hate people if he sat and talked with them, so on the day of the game he did everything he could to avoid a face-to-face encounter with Krueger. Then, just before the game, as Kramer was walking down the tunnel to the field, he heard a voice behind him. It was Krueger, calling out in his characteristic Texas accent, "Is Joe Kramer thayuh?" Kramer muttered to himself, "How can I hate a man with an accent like that?" Third-ear-listening had spoiled Kramer's plans.

Toward the end of World War II social scientists were surprised and in many instances delighted with Dr. Carl Rogers' new psychotherapeutic counseling technique. Whereas past authorities had emphasized the intellectual or volitional aspects of personality, here was a technique highlighting the emotional aspects. A basic proposition of this theory was that it lay much greater stress upon the emotional, feeling aspects of a situation, than upon the intellectual.

Rogers emphasized that most failures in life came because people gain emotional satisfaction from them; therefore, the task is to work directly on the emotions. The skill of the counselor in these situations lay in understanding the emotions of the client. He spent hours becoming able to perceive emotions and to reflect them to the client. If he were to be successful, he must be a third-ear listener *par excellence.*

Learning the Skill

One way to learn to appreciate third-ear-listening is to participate in the third-ear exercise. You can do this with your family or a group of like-minded people interested in developing interpersonal skills.

Prepare slips of paper for all the members of the group. Simple drawings of smiling, frowning, serious, sad, and blank faces or circles with the appropriate words in them should appear on each slip. (See the illustration at the top of page 99.)

Each member of the group should have a number of slips of paper equal to the number of members in the group, plus one for himself. On each piece of paper he writes the name of one of the group members. This slip is to be the means of his indicating the emotion he perceives the contributor to be experiencing.

Example:

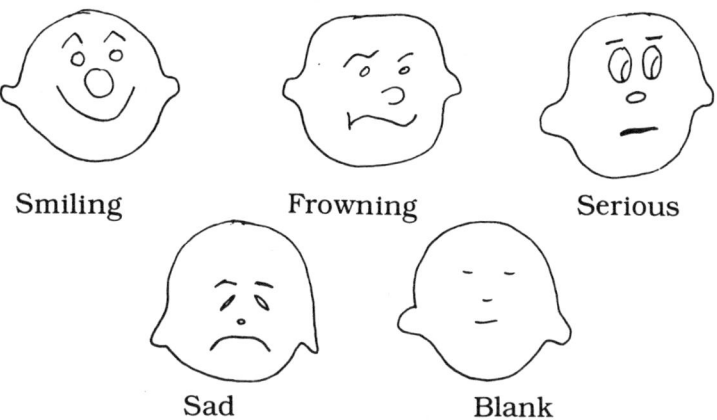

Smiling   Frowning   Serious

Sad   Blank

The leader of the group announces a topic for discussion, preferably something controversial such as: "Abortion should be available on demand."

As each individual participates in the discussion, the other members take careful note, not only of what the contributor is *saying*, but of the way that he appears to *feel*. Using the slip labeled with the contributor's name, members mark the appropriate face.

After the leader concludes the exercise, he puts his own name on a slip and checks a diagram to indicate how he felt during the discussion.

After all the papers have been checked, the leader calls on a member and asks, "Jim, tell us how you perceived that Joe felt." The others follow in turn. At the conclusion Joe reveals how he *really* felt during his contribution.

Let these questions serve as the basis for discussion:

1. Can we really judge the way people feel?
2. What are the indications that a person is emotionally overwrought?

3. How are the body and voice involved?
4. How can we best help people who are emotionally upset?

Learning third-ear-listening is difficult, but it may be one of the most rewarding of all listening techniques.

13
Body-listening

"A body you have prepared for me; . . . I have come to do your will, O God" (Heb. 10:5, 7 NIV).

I once attended a lecture by a famous sociologist who listened with his ears, and possibly with his eyes, but not with his body. At the conclusion of the presentation, after announcing that he was as willing to hear as to speak, he invited the group members to express their opinions and ask questions about the subject under discussion.

This scientist's reactions to the people who spoke were a fascinating study in themselves. He turned his big black eyes upon the somewhat verbose questioner with a beady stare as if to lull him into a hypnotic trance and, hopefully, silence. If a participant persisted, the sociologist's black, bushy eyebrows began a rhythmic movement, like two gyrating caterpillars. His rather large red lips shaped unspoken words, occasionally reinforced by strange incoherent sounds. Ham-like hands reached out in mesmeric movements.

When he spoke, his words were, "Go on," but every response of his body shouted, "Keep quiet and let me talk!" He didn't know it, but his body was not listening.

One of the most interesting sidelights of a fascinating life is the means of communication used by the genius of the communications world, Thomas Alva Edison. Edison's first wife, Mary Stillwell, died in 1884. Two years later he remarried—a marriage preceded by a most unusual courtship. By this time Edison had lost his hearing and had developed skill in using Morse code. As his relationship with Nina Miller grew, he taught her to use the code. Spending long periods of time together, they became adept at tapping out messages on each other's hands.

When Edison finally decided to "pop the question," he used the familiar Morse code. Nina responded with what Edison called "an easy word to send by telegraphic signals—yes."

On their honeymoon trip, traveling by train through the White Mountains, Edison and his new bride carried on a sugary, newlywed, pet-name conversation despite the presence of three other people in the carriage. They accomplished this rather unusual feat by tapping out the telegraphic code on each other's hands!

My wife was delighted with the Edisons and their system of body communication. She has always had a secret fear that a prowler would enter our home at night and that I, being the lighter sleeper, would awaken but be unable to let her know of the intruder. When I suggested that I give a plain old everyday nudge, she expressed her apprehension that the message might come across to her as: "Give me some more blanket." So, I taught her a simple signal. I would tap out on the most convenient portion of her body, *dit-dit-dit, dah-dah-dah, dit-dit-dit,* which of course is SOS. This example of body listening has made her feel more secure.

How to "Soften Up" a Person

Some of our best studies in body communication come from the field of negotiations. Many negotiators make verbal statements which have hidden meanings. From videotapes which have been made of negotiating sessions, we know that many body movements have distinctive meanings.

The techniques of body listening make up the acrostic SOFTEN—

S MILE
O PEN POSTURE
F ORWARD LEAN
T OUCH
E YE CONTACT
N OD

Smile. Carrying on communication with a sullen-faced individual is altogether different from talking with a person with a winning smile. The smile which is most effective is sometimes called an "upper smile," in which the listener exposes the upper incisors while maintaining eye-to-eye contact with speaker. This smile is probably the most important single factor in establishing rapport between two people.

In doing a television series I participated in a small weekly segment. When the taping took place I had to spend a lot of time sitting on the set, awaiting my turn to be on camera. The camera would sometimes be focused on me when I was not expecting it, as a fellow participant spoke and I listened. Periodically would come the dread words, "Cut! . . . Dr. Drakeford, lighten up!"

"Lightening up" or smiling is a vital aspect of the total listening process.

Open Posture. The gesture for defensiveness, defiance, and withdrawal is an arms-crossed posture. In contrast, upturned palms indicate sincerity and openness. The person who is listening with his body will avoid crossed arms and maintain an open posture.

Forward lean. The body listener who leans forward, toward the speaker, gives the impression of movement toward him or her, and intense interest in what is being said. One who sits leaning back, one leg crossed in a figure-four position, with both hands clasped behind his head conveys a message of superiority, smugness, and authority.

Touch. Dolly Parton is a superb communicator, both onstage and on film. As Southern as black-eyed peas, poured into dresses that accentuate her hourglass figure, topped with exaggerated but attractive wigs, Miss Dolly comes across as sweet as molasses. But what is she really like in person? An interviewer has noted the way Dolly talks or "bubbles." The attractive woman's hands are constantly busy, touching the writer, lightly caressing to make a point. Dolly likes to touch people. As the star readily admits, "If I see somebody I want to hug, they don't have to want to hug me back, but that's not gonna stop me from being who *I* am. Lots of people envy me 'cause I'm able to reach out to touch somebody's face or to squeeze them or to say, 'I just love you to death.'" Dolly sees her touching as communicating her love and adds, "If it's not right to love, then what do we have?" What indeed?

Eye contact. Turning the head to look directly at a speaker is the primary indication of attention. After the announcement of the new budget, the controller of a large organization found himself faced with a long line of protesters. In an effort to gain his attention, one department head sent his prettiest female employee to talk with the controller on his behalf. The controller countered this tactic by looking out the window all the time the advocate was making her presentation. "He never looked at me!" she said in frustration. "I felt as if I were in a room of a deserted house."

Nod. In the chapter of head-listening (Chapter Nine), we have already noted the effectiveness of nodding, a listening technique.

The Total Listener in Action

Total listening might be described as the activity in which the listener goes to work to utilize every part of his body—his mouth, his eyes, etc.—to make the other person feel loved, valued, and worthwhile. Frank Capra, the celebrated movie producer, spent some time with Franklin D. Roosevelt, at that time President of the United States, and described the way in which F.D.R. entered into a conversation with him.

> . . . with a big friendly smile, and the glint of intense interest in his sparkling eyes, he would encourage you to talk about yourself, your family, your work, anything. "Well, I declare!" he'd exclaim after you'd made some inane statement. By little laughs, and goads, and urgings such as "Really? Tell me more!" . . . "Well, what do you know!" . . . "Same thing's happened to me dozens of times!" . . . "Oh, that's fascinating!" . . . his warmth would change you from a stuttering milquetoast to an articulate raconteur.

Small wonder President Roosevelt, the man of the people, was able to marshall the forces of democracy against the tyranny of the Axis Powers.

Body listening will help you to be as effective in your field as the president was in his.

Targets for
Listening Skills

14

The Public Relations Technique Nobody Mentions

"Be a good listener. Encourage others to talk about themselves." —Dale Carnegie

Jean was an attractive girl—tastefully dressed, with soft, fair hair and the loveliest, pale blue eyes. In addition to her natural beauty she possessed the rare ingredient of extreme intelligence. Every time the university honors list appeared, Jean's name was sure to be at or near the top.

Many of the girls at the university she attended were more beautiful and more expensively dressed, and her intelligence could have deterred the attention of males who liked to feel that they possessed superior masculine wisdom.

But Jean had more men trying to date her than almost any other girl. They gathered around her like bees at a honey pot. At social functions the men gravitated toward her, frequently leaving her equally attractive sisters in order to spend time in her charming company.

Deeply religious, Jean preferred "church dates." She attended every service of the church and generally came escorted by an athlete or some other campus notable.

As her pastor, and a psychologist as well, I felt this psychological phenomenon was worthy of investigation. I made arrangements for Jean to come by my office for a conference.

Formalities done with, I said, "Now, Jean, tell me about yourself—where you come from, the high school you attended, your major field of study, and what you plan to be."

Jean turned those big blue eyes on me. "Why, Pastor, I have lived such an ordinary existence! You have traveled the world. Why don't you tell me something about yourself?"

Naturally, I wanted to help the girl. So I launched into an account of my experiences while she hung on my every word. And the intensity of those eyes was so appealing that I once forgot what I was saying!

I didn't learn much about Jean's background, field of study, or ambitions, but I discovered her secret. Her unusual attractiveness lay in her capacity to *listen*.

Listen—to Develop Charm

Some time after my encounter with Jean I read a magazine article in which the writer told of some memorable advice from her mother. The daughter, preparing for her first big social event, was taken aside by her mother, who had grown up in the Southern-belle tradition. The mother offered some wise counsel regarding conversation with her date. "Try to get your beau to do the talking, my dear. Most men can't resist a girl who asks leading questions and pays attention to their answers!"

It was a simple but very appropriate suggestion for the apprehensive debutante. If this were in any way typical of the guidance Southern mothers give their daughters, it might be more than half the reason for the traditional charm of the Southern girl.

This wise bit of feminine strategy dates all the way back to the Queen of Sheba, and probably accounts for her conquest of King Solomon. "She communed with him of all that was in her heart. And Solomon told her all her questions'" (2 Chron. 9:1–2).

John Wesley, the founder of Methodism, was very attractive to women, who delighted in his presence. But few of them ever struck a responsive chord with him. One who did was Sophy Hopkey.

Wesley met Sophy in Georgia and was immediately attracted to her. A year after the pathetic conclusion of their relationship he wrote a frank account of the remarkable story, revealing at least one reason why Sophy cast such a spell over him.

In his description of the sweet young girl he says, "Another thing I was much pleased in her was, that whenever we were conversing or reading, there was such a stillness in her whole behavior, scarce stirring hand or foot, that she seemed to be, all but her attention, dead!"

A good proportion of Sophy's appeal lay in her *listening heart.*

Listen—to Inspire Confidence

When a disturbed and troubled person plucks up enough courage to visit a psychotherapist, he frequently approaches the encounter with fear and apprehension. Seated for the first time in the office, he makes a mental evaluation, outwardly smiling, inwardly wondering, *Why ever on earth did I come here?* He speculates whether or not this is just a futile venture.

If any type of counseling is to take place, it is vital that rapport be established early in the relationship. *Rapport* is the clinician's word which means "a harmonious or sympathetic relation or connection."

There are many factors which go into establishing rapport, the most important of which is listening. As the counselor listens, the counselee's confidence is built, and he is able to get involved in the counseling process.

Listen—to Win Friends and Influence People

Few men have been more successful in the field of human relations than Dale Carnegie. His book, *How to Win Friends and Influence People*, was a best seller and is still widely read. The organization Carnegie founded continues to flourish and propagate his ideas, long after his death. Busy executives take time out and pay considerable sums of money to take his courses.

Carnegie's book tells of his attending a party where a celebrated botanist was a guest of honor. Carnegie's questions about the famous man's field of study launched the scientist into a near-monologue that lasted throughout the evening.

When it was time to go, the botanist told his host that Carnegie was "a most interesting conversationalist," although Carnegie had hardly spoken a word.

"I had listened intently," said Carnegie. "I had listened because I was genuinely interested."

Though discussion of Carnegie's techniques generally centers on *speaking* skills, he was obviously also concerned with listening skills.

In a recent television reminiscence, Bob Hope told of climbing into a New York taxi and giving the driver his instructions. As soon as the cabby realized his passenger's identity, he burst into song, continuing until they reached their destination. Then he cast an inquiring glance in Hope's direction.

Hope opined, "You've got a good voice. Why don't you get yourself an agent?"

The cabby waved off the fare with, "Forget it. You listened!"

Will that cab driver tell his children and grandchildren, "I met Bob Hope"?

I rather fancy his story will be, "Bob Hope listened to me!"

La Rochefoucauld said, "We usually forgive those who bore us, but we never forgive those whom we bore." He who would establish good relationships with people must learn to listen to them.

A Critical Listening Incident

You are with a group of people on whom you'd like to make an impression. A friend has the center of the floor, and all sorts of puns on his remarks keep occurring to you. Do you—
    a. resist the temptation to come out with them?
    b. demonstrate your wit and amuse the others by making them?
    c. whisper them to the person beside you?

Answer: a. You have to be both generous and possessed of willpower not to steal a little thunder in situations like this, but you'll feel better for keeping mum. And, you never gain, even in prestige, by deflating another!

15
A Forgotten Factor in Leadership

When we listen, we pay the speaker the highest of tributes, and gain a means of inducing other people to give us their loyalty and support. —J.W.D.

A Midwestern plant experienced a severe quality problem with a mass-produced delicate mechanism. A swarm of experts—design engineers, quality-control men, and maintenance men—descended on the assembly line, but found no immediate solution to the problem. Worried about the rising rate of rejects and customer complaints, top management finally called in a management consulting firm. Eventually they identified and resolved the problem—one of dust control.

About a month later, the personnel director received a jolt when a promising young assembler reported that he was quitting his job. When asked his reasons for terminating, the young man evaded the questions. But the personnel director, sensing something important, probed and listened.

Eventually the story unfolded: The assembler hadn't been absolutely sure, but he had thought that he had known the answer to the quality problem that the experts had so desperately sought a short time earlier. As it developed, his hunch had been right.

"If you thought you knew the answer," the puzzled director asked, "why didn't you tell us?"

"I tried to tell the foreman. I tried to tell the design engineer. I stopped trying because they made me feel like a jerk. They wouldn't listen."

Failure to listen had cost a company thousands of dollars. But even more crucial was the damage to a young man's morale and sense of worth.

This incident highlights a factor in leadership that is often overlooked—listening.

The great corporations are now learning to listen to their rank and file employees. This new attitude was recently highlighted in an article entitled "Lending an Ear" in the economy and business section of a national news magazine. Companies are instituting programs with catchy titles, such as "Expressline," "Speak Up," and "Open Door," which allow employees to make direct contact with management by a hot line or through the mail.

Some of these companies have gone to unusual lengths to encourage employees to let their bosses know how they feel. According to one plan, the employee's inquiry is written out on a special form which is mailed to an outside post office box, retyped, and presented to the appropriate executive, with the promise that there will be a reply from responsible persons, including the company chairman, within ten days. A professor at Columbia's business school has applauded these new efforts and makes the point that this new attitude is "part of the general concern for ways to improve productivity."

There are some good reasons listening is important in leading.

The Listening Leader Is Influential

The Bolshevik takeover in Russia reached a crisis point when the revolutionary dictator, Vladimir Lenin, was hospitalized with a stroke, and it became evident a new leader would have to be chosen. There were two logical contenders for the position. They represented two entirely different approaches to the task of leadership. One was a talker; the other, a listener.

The talker was Leon Trotsky, a flamboyant orator and brilliant organizer. Pictures of Trotsky show him clad in his greatcoat, standing before large gatherings of people, inspiring them with his speeches.

Josef Stalin, on the other hand, had a different approach. Stalin's biographer says the most striking thing about him was that there was nothing striking about him. Handicapped by his Georgian accent, he was never a very effective public speaker and realized he had to concentrate on other areas. While Trotsky was out haranguing huge crowds, Stalin sat and listened. His tongue was still, but his mind worked furiously.

The odds seemed against Stalin. Lenin had said in his testament, "I propose to the comrades to find a way to remove Stalin." Lenin's wife, who exercised considerable influence in the upper echelons of the party, was also hostile to him.

But Stalin, through skillful manipulation, had Trotsky sidetracked, exiled, and finally killed by the assassin's ax.

Stalin's listening technique paid off. He had established friendships and relationships with multitudes of party hacks and thus had paved the way for the final intrigues opening the pathway to leadership. The listener had defeated the talker.

If this is true of a dictatorship, it is of greater importance for a democracy.

Calvin Coolidge, always a man of few words, followed a political career that ultimately led to the White House. A somewhat voluble woman once related to him that she had bet a friend she would get at least three words of conversation out of the President. Still casually looking the other way, he quietly responded, "You lose." Small wonder he was nicknamed "Silent Cal."

Assessing the peculiar skills of this taciturn man, his biographer says, he "was Northampton's champion listener; listened his way into all the offices the town would give him." He continued to listen through his Vice Presidency and Presidency of the United States.

In his book *The Art of Listening,* published in 1958, Dominick Barbara used an illustration by making reference to a sign on the wall of a senator's office in Washington, D.C. It read: "You Ain't Learnin' Nothin' While You're Talkin'."

The then-comparatively obscure senator was Lyndon B. Johnson of Texas—later to be President of the United States.

Although he once taught speech in Texas schools, even his most enthusiastic admirers would not venture to call President Johnson a great orator. His strength apparently lay in his personal face-to-face encounters with members of Congress.

Hourly employees of one large plant said of their favorite foreman: "He listens. I can talk to him." They equated his performance with his listening ability.

The Listening Leader Is Inspirational

One authority in the field of leadership speaks about the necessity of the leader's making an "effective show of devotion." Such a display may take the form of a statement of appreciation by the leader, but by far the most effective way to do it will be to indicate a willingness to listen to what his followers have to say.

The late Norman Rockwell told of his meeting with General Dwight D. Eisenhower. The General, prior to his presidential campaign, was returning from the Republican convention and stopped off at Denver for a brief vacation. The *Saturday Evening Post* arranged for him to sit for a painting.

While the artist found the General warm, friendly, and cooperative, with an expressive face, he tells about his clearest impression of all.

"The general and I didn't discuss politics or the campaign. Mostly we talked about painting and fishing. But what I remember most about the hour and a half I spent with him was the way he gave me all his attention. He was listening to me and talking to me, just as if he hadn't a care in the world, hadn't been through the trials of a political convention, wasn't on the brink of a presidential campaign."

Once again, we see the hallmark of a great leader—knowing how to listen, and, in doing so, winning a friend and an admirer.

There is a sense in which, by listening to people, we can earn credits that will forever put them in debt to us. My friend Hillis Small, an expert in business management, sells his services for handsome fees. One night at church he met an attractive young couple, Harry and Joan Simpson by name. Husband Harry invited Hillis and his wife to have dinner with them on the following Thursday.

The meal, which proved to be equal to Hillis' anticipation, was concluded, and his host asked Hillis about his work. At this particular time Hillis was handling a difficult situation and needed little encouragement to pour out his story of the frustration he had experienced.

His host was exemplary in his conduct. He gave

Hillis his complete attention, refused to let either his or Hillis' wife break the train of conversation, and when at last Hillis concluded, he felt warm and grateful to his host.

Only then did his host say, "Hillis, I have a small problem, nothing as complex as the one you're working on. Let me tell you about it."

Hillis listened to the man's story and then came up with a recommendation of which he said, "I *gave* him what would have cost him $600 if he'd called me in for a consultation."

Knowing rather tight-fisted Hillis wasn't given to squandering his time and money, I asked a rather obvious question, "What caused you to give away 600 bucks?"

Hillis responded, "Well, he'd listened to all my griping. I felt I *owed* him something."

The Listening Leader Is Open-minded

When Charles Nordhoff, a widely-experienced newspaper reporter and investigator, visited the Oneida community, he marveled at the way this society ran its affairs, particularly in the use of a type of radical group therapy known as "criticism."

The procedure was fairly simple. A good community member volunteered to be the subject, and the whole company gathered in the meeting place. Then as the subject sat in the midst, the community members took turns telling him what they considered to be his faults and failings.

From Nordhoff's description of one of these meetings, it is obvious that the community member who exposed himself to this experience suffered quite an ordeal. But apparently they thought it beneficial. Nordhoff pondered the problems of living at such close quarters and came to the conclusion that "criticism" was a near-perfect solution.

Most of us feel a stinging blow to our self-love

when someone points out our faults, failings, or foibles, especially in the presence of others. Yet it is of the utmost importance that we know how we appear to other people. The famous Scottish poet breathed the prayer that contains such a vital truth:

> O wad some Power the giftie gie us
> To see oursels as ithers see us!
> It wad frae monie a blunder free us.

Few humans would really pray this prayer themselves, even though the poet observer points up how badly we really need a critic. Airing criticism will often defuse it, causing the critic to become an admirer.

All of us get criticism. The trick is in learning to take it. If criticism is unjust and unfair, the critic may be disarmed. On the other hand, justified criticism teaches us something. We can gain both ways by listening.

The Listening Leader Is Communicative

George Orwell's book *1984* depicts a regime in which all men are equal—but some are "more equal than others." The dictator is Big Brother, and in every home there is an all-seeing eye. Constant warning that "Big Brother is watching" is whispered from one to the other.

In a democracy the relationship of the leader and people might better by symbolized by an all-hearing ear in every home. Then the matter is less what the leader thinks of people than what the people think of the leader.

Near the conclusion of a press conference with President Johnson, one newsman asked, "Mr. President, do you know what the pollsters have found out about you?"

Did he know?

Without consulting a single note, he was able to

quote what the various polls had discovered. He knew the percentage points of people's assessment of his foreign policy, domestic policy, his personal popularity, and half a dozen other aspects of his administration. Obviously public opinion polls were of first-rate importance to him.

The modern politician has a listening ear, and through his mail and public opinion polls he is paying close attention to what his followers are feeling and thinking. He may even learn something.

One expert says: "Good communication is an exchange. The communicator must constantly take the temperature of the people with whom he is communicating."

Thor Heyerdahl concentrated more on the mysteries of human migration than on listening; but in the course of a scientific expedition to Easter Island, Heyerdahl's party attempted to grapple with the mysteries of the enormous statues—tall as houses and heavy as boxcars—that lay strewn around. How had primitive people with no engineering techniques managed to raise and position these tremendous chunks of carved stone?

Though the mayor of the island, Don Pedro, was a somewhat talkative individual, Heyerdahl questioned his credibility. When asked how the statues were moved from one part of the island to the other, he often smiled and said, "They walked."

One day out of the clear blue sky, the scientist again popped the question to the mayor, "Don't you know how these giants were raised?"

"Yes, Señor, I know; there's nothing to it."

Somewhat skeptical that this might be more native braggadocio, the investigator proceeded to query him; but the mayor continued to maintain stoutly that he could raise a statue himself, providing he had enough labor to help him.

So Heyerdahl commissioned him to do just that. Employing the services of a large group of fellow citizens, the mayor obtained three long wooden poles which they used as levers. They combined their efforts to raise the head of the statue a fraction of an inch, while helpers pushed stones under it.

They continued the process—alternately levering and pushing more stones, gradually building up the stone supports—until the statue stood upright.

Scarcely daring to believe his own eyes, the researcher turned to the mayor and reminded him of all the investigators who had tried to discover the secret of how the statues were erected and asked, "Why didn't you tell all those people?"

The mayor responded, "No one asked me."

There are many people who know a lot more than we even give them credit for knowing.

In the year 1981 the world was shocked by the news that the president of Egypt, Anwar Sadat, the dynamic leader who had almost single-handedly pushed Egypt into international prominence, had been assassinated. Sadat was a magnificent speaker, not so much in terms of a flowing fluency, but because his speech was tempered with those friendly "ers" and "ahs" that seemed to evoke confidence in his hearers. The world was amazed when he offered to make a gesture toward his implacable foes, the Israelis, and visit Jerusalem as a demonstration of the way in which an Arab leader could build bridges into the Western world.

Following Sadat's untimely death, his closest aide and heir apparent, fifty-one-year-old Hosni Mubarak, was confirmed by the electorate as the new president. Immediately upon assuming office, he called for unity using a typical Arabian figure of speech, "We are all in the same caravan." Many speculated as to whether Mubarak could continue to offer the same dynamic leadership of his country as had his predecessor. A capable speaker who lacks Sadat's charisma, Mubarak brings another communication skill. "He has an important trait. He listens, and in this part of the world we need a leader who listens."

Too often the busy executive says, "I don't have time to listen carefully." The only reply is, "You don't have time *not* to listen carefully!"

Remember, the greatest of all leaders said, "He that hath ears to hear, let him hear" (Matt. 11:15).

Listening Test for Executives

Read the ten questions below and, for each of them, please check yes or no.

1. As people talk to you, do you find it difficult to keep your mind on the subject at hand, or to keep from taking mental excursions from the line of thought conveyed? Yes ☐ No ☐
2. Do you listen primarily for facts, rather than ideas, when someone is speaking? Yes ☐ No ☐
3. Do certain words, phrases, or ideas so prejudice you against a speaker that you cannot listen objectively to what is being conveyed? Yes ☐ No ☐
4. When you are puzzled or annoyed by what someone says, do you try to get the question straightened out immediately? Yes ☐ No ☐
5. If you feel it would take too much time and effort to understand something, do you go out of your way to avoid hearing about it? Yes ☐ No ☐
6. Do you deliberately turn your thoughts to other subjects when you believe a speaker will have nothing particularly interesting to say? Yes ☐ No ☐
7. Can you tell by a person's appearance and delivery that he won't have anything worthwhile to say? Yes ☐ No ☐
8. When somebody is talking to you, do you try to make him think you are paying attention when you are not? Yes ☐ No ☐

9. When you are lisening to someone, are you easily distracted by outside sights and sounds? Yes ☐ No ☐
10. If you really want to remember what someone is saying, do you try to write down most of his discourse? Yes ☐ No ☐

16
New Medicine for Sick Marriages

If there is to be a rewarding marriage relationship, there must be adequate assimilative communication. —J.W.D.

You can imagine the surprise of a Winter Park, Florida family on Mother's Day of 1981, when they returned from church to find that their beautiful house had completely disappeared!

The house, along with six expensive sports cars that happened to be parked in the vicinity, was the victim of a strange Florida phenomenon known as a "sinkhole." Where the house had once stood was a gaping hole, 1000 feet wide and 125 feet deep. The hole continued to widen, eating up a roadway, two business, and the public swimming pool. The owner of a $40,000 automobile, who had left his car for a tune-up, found it had taken a turn down. With irrepressible logic, he chartered a large helicopter in a futile attempt to rescue the rapidly disappearing vehicle. Residents crossed their fingers as the hole slowly continued to widen.

The sinkhole attracted many sightseers and caused much speculation as to its future. One practical-minded engineer suggested it might make a good garbage dump, and, once refilled, a new building lot. However, its enormous size meant that many years would be required to fill it and make it into something useful. Another city official projected the possibility that, if the hole were filled with water, it could become yet another lake.

There have been speculations as to the cause of sinkholes. The most logical seems to be that the constant pumping up of underground water has depleted the aquifer (supplier) and has left large cavities, once abrim with water, completely empty. The ceiling of the cavity, no longer supported by the water, collapses to fill the space, causing the surface above to subside and leave a large void.

The sudden and unexpected collapse of the house with an apparently secure foundation is parallel to home life today. Certain elements deep in the foundation of a family help it maintain its equilibrium. Communication is the aquifer of family foundations. Channels of communication provide fluid, but vital, undergirding for the family. As these are blocked off and dry up, dire consequences result.

The collapse of the house in Florida was the climax of a situation which had been deteriorating for a long time. The same is true of families. They are not destroyed in a single moment. They need some ways to preserve the undergirding channels of communication so that the situation might be saved.

Some Communication Brings Deterioration

If we use the generally accepted idea that communication is verbal alone, we will soon discover that certain types of talking only help to bring about deterioration of a marriage relationship.

1. *Nagging*—The communication technique called "nagging" is a perversion of the long-cherished educational idea that repetition breeds retention. Unfortunately, however, verbiage is by no means an indicator of successful communication. Pliny the Elder once admitted, "I am writing you at length, because I do not have time to write a short letter." The Lord's Prayer contains fifty-six words; the Gettysburg Address, 266; the Declaration of Independence, 300; and the government directive on cabbage prices, 29,911.

Nagging is not only ineffective, but can also be counterproductive. The word *nag* has been defined as "to torment by persistent faultfinding, complaints, or importunities." The Oxford Dictionary adds some interesting overtones to the definition, stating that *to nag* means "to gnaw, bite, nibble." Those who are continually nagged may become defensive or completely ignore the nagger.

Another attempt to influence people by using expressive communication techniques is the use of the "put-down." The user of put-downs often has the personal satisfaction of having made a clever response in words such as:

- "I know I'm wasting my breath, but . . ."
- "No one in his right mind could believe that . . ."
- "Everybody knows that . . ."
- "Where did you get that dumb idea?"
- "It really isn't any of my business, but . . ."
- "Why do you always think you know more than anybody else?"
- "If you're not interested in hearing the facts . . ."
- "Are you trying to be funny?"
- "I don't want to hurt your feelings, but . . ."

- "If I tell you something, will you promise not to get mad?"

There are two possible attitudes toward put-downs. We can cherish the moment of ego inflation in having been clever. Or we can take a long look at ourselves and ask if this will really strengthen our relationships. Forgoing the ego trip may help us move toward better interaction.

2. *Interrupting*—Still another expressive communication method used by husbands and wives is interrupting. The nicest and politest of people, who will go to much trouble to be courteous and polite when talking to friends and business acquaintances, suddenly become positively bad-mannered when breaking in on a spouse.

Let's eavesdrop on Phillip and June Pedemont. Phillip loves to tell a funny story but, like many of us, he has a limited repertoire. Those he knows, he tells fairly well, and they sound pretty good to everyone but June.

Phillip begins, "Have you heard that story about the Baptist preacher who went to the circus . . . ?"

"Oh, Phillip, do you have to tell that old story again? It's got whiskers on it."

Phillip hesitates, thoroughly deflated. If he goes on, it will be with a gnawing feeling of uncertainty and a grim suspicion that they have probably heard the tale a dozen times over. His wife, trying to save her friends, has effectively cut her husband down to size.

Who cares if June has heard the story twenty-five times over? A musician may play a piece of music a hundred times, becoming better and better because of his practice. And Phillip was not really telling the story for *June*.

It is sometimes claimed that the pattern of German family life was set by Martin Luther, a former monk who married a former nun. Their marriage relationship was an open book to the horde of student boarders who filled their large house.

Many of the students kept a record of every event in the reformer's life, including numerous examples of the way Martin and Katherine communicated with each other.

On one occasion as they sat eating their meal, Martin, in answer to a student's question, launched into a lengthy response. His wife voiced her mounting concern about the meal she had so carefully prepared, now becoming cold and unappetizing.

The exasperated husband replied, "I wish that women would repeat the Lord's Prayer before opening their mouths!"

Martin himself was not above interrupting. In one petulant moment he interjected a sarcastic comment about his wife's prayer for rain: "Yes, why not, Lord? We have persecuted Thy Word and killed Thy saints. We have deserved well of Thee."

Yet, from all the information of Luther's life, we know that he loved Katherine very deeply. There were moments, however, when he felt the frustration of his marriage relationship.

Husbands and wives must constantly remember they are teammates, not rivals. In any group situation, a husband and wife can have fun by playing the conversational game as fellow team members. Here are some hints:

- Never, never, never interrupt your spouse. Remember an interruption can be devastating. Resist every urge to interrupt, and listen.
- Help your spouse to save face. People often make foolish statements which are obviously incorrect. You don't have to correct your partner—keep listening.
- Be as pleasant and friendly with your husband or wife as you would with a stranger, and don't forget to listen.

- People are always more interested in themselves than they are in you—so listen.
- As your spouse talks, formulate a question that will encourage him or her and then listen for the answer.
- Play conversational tennis, seeing how adept you can become in hitting the conversational ball back to your mate and waiting for a return by listening.
- Watch for warning signals; be sensitive to your partner's reactions. If you are not doing so well, try listening for a while.

The Other Woman

One of the most predictable features of a deteriorating marriage relationship is the attraction of either husband or wife to a third person. The really surprising aspect of these situations is that it is more likely to be a descending than an ascending infatuation.

Jim Heffner is a capable and successful businessman. Apparently happily married, he has an attractive wife and two lovely children. His wife Jean takes her situation for granted, vaguely aware that she has a very satisfactory marriage. She speaks openly to her friends about the reliability of "dear old Jim."

Mrs. Heffner is shocked beyond words when she accidently discovers her husband is having an affair. Further investigation indicates the "other woman" is neat and nicely dressed, but not nearly as attractive as Jean, and certainly no glamorous sexpot or obvious seducer of married men.

After a period of blaming everything on her husband and "that woman," Mrs. Heffner finally begins to ask herself where she has failed. In answer to an inquiry as to what the other woman had that she lacked, Jim, her husband, replies, "She was genuinely interested in me. She sat and listened to what I had to say."

Mrs. Heffner is humiliated but is finally able to see that she was far too preoccupied with the children, PTA, her clubs, and a whole host of other interests which kept her from taking much notice of her husband and his work. Above everything else, she had failed in the perfectly simple technique of listening.

It might all come down to a lesson in economics. Most mothers instruct their daughters to make sure they pay all the housekeeping bills; and both husband and wife may be meticulously careful in paying the electric, gas, telephone, and water bills and taxes, while leaving unpaid the most important debt of all. Husbands and wives must pay *attention* to each other!

Marriage communication means giving the other person time to speak. A ham radio operator established contact with a boyhood friend of mine, now about ten thousand miles distant. It was a thrill to hear his voice, but I soon discovered there were no opportunities for interruption. Not until my friend in far-off Australia had finished talking and had turned the radio channel over to me with the word *over*, could I speak.

A good listener must always give the other person time. There must come a moment when, like the radio operator, he signals, "Over." Only then will adequate communication take place.

Action for Reestablishing Communication

Try these steps in reestablishing the communication process:
- Acknowledge the importance and meaning of communication in marriage.
- Face the fact that *lack of listening* is probably the greatest point of failure in most marriages.

- Quit blaming. Remember, a man or woman is never stronger than when admitting his or her weaknesses.
- Settle on a specific period of time to listen to each other. Arrange for a minimum of distractions. If the situation is sensitive, make a division of time: Ten minutes for her, ten for him, the rest of the time for exchange. Agree there will be no interrupting of each other, no flying off the handle, no sulking.
- Try signing and living by the following communication contract.

Communication Contract

We the undersigned, being parties to this agreement, each hereby agree:

I AGREE communication is the basis of a good marriage relationship, and I will embark on a course of action to build up our interpersonal communications.

I AGREE that I will listen to your remarks and comments without interrupting you. When it is my turn to talk, I expect the same courtesy.

I AGREE that I will first look for things to criticize about myself before I criticize you. Before I complain to you, I will name some fault of mine that, if corrected, would make me a better marriage partner.

I AGREE that sex is a significant level of communication and that I have a sexual obligation in our marriage. Our sexual relations will never be used as a means of reward or punishment.

I AGREE that direct communication proceeds best on a verbal level, and I will not try to send messages by banging doors or other nonverbal means.

I AGREE not to use silence as a means of punishing or defying you but as a means of encouraging you to express yourself.

I AGREE not to expect miracles in the improvement of our marriage. There is a great deal you need to know about me and I about you before we can consider ourselves truly married. But I will make every effort toward mutual knowledge and understanding.

I AGREE on the assumption that example is the most persuasive form of argument known to man, that I will diligently seek to improve myself and my communication skills so I can grow into a continually better model of a marriage mate.

Husband _____ Wife _____
Date _____

Mastering the Art of Listening

17

Understanding Fallacies About Listening

The idea that listening is a normal development of our perceptive processes involves several basic false assumptions. —J.W.D.

Fallacy 1. *Intelligent people are good listeners.* Many maintain that those with a high intelligence level will automatically be able to listen and comprehend well. But because they have a pretty good self-image, they often feel that there is no need to be concerned about such a skill. In fact, they may feel that studying listening skills may be an acknowledgment of a low level of intelligence.

There is no evidence to show this is so.

Intelligence may, however, *hinder* listening. The very intelligent often become impatient with the slower-speaking individual. Because he can't be bothered waiting around for him to complete his message, he tunes him out.

Listening skills, like any other, must be learned, practiced, and developed—regardless of intelligence level.

Fallacy 2. Good hearing means good listening. Since listening is often confused with hearing, it is assumed hearing problems are the reason some people don't listen. However, investigation shows that many with perfectly good hearing are poor listeners.

What we do with our hearing equipment is the all-important consideration. We may use excellent equipment for the wrong purpose and so be poor listeners.

Fallacy 3. Our everyday listening builds our skill. We have concluded that constant listening experiences improve listening skills, and that we learn to listen in much the same way that we learn to walk. Unfortunately, though, some children do not learn to walk correctly, and frequently require correction. The same is true of listening. Practice does not always make perfect, if we practice our mistakes!

Fallacy 4. Reading develops our listening ability. Because we acquire much of our knowledge through the receptive or assimilative skill of reading, we may assume that developing this ability makes us better listeners. But there are considerable differences between reading and listening. At its best, reading is a solitary experience, requiring isolation, in order to concentrate on a book, and may even foster an antisocial attitude. The traditional view of the librarian is her reprimanding any person with effrontery enough to talk with a fellow library user. In contrast, listening is a social experience always involving at least two people.

Moreover, the reader chooses his own pace, taking up or laying down the book when he has the urge, but the listener must follow the speaker's pace. If the listener does not seize the extemporaneous speech and take possession of it in the moment of its birth, then it dies and is lost to him. While there is considerable evidence that listening skills may increase reading ability, there is no evidence that good reading skills increase listening ability.

Fallacy 5. Electronic communication makes listening obsolete. Even the United States Army, with its highly developed technological communication skills, has had to face communication problems as it struggled with getting a message through all the listeners in the chain of command. The following tongue-in-cheek report in an army communication illustrates the problem.

One day the commander issued the following order to his executive officer:

"Tomorrow evening, at approximately 2000 hours, Halley's Comet will be visible in this area, an event which occurs only once every seventy-five years. Have the men fall out in the battalion area in fatigues, and I will explain this rare phenomenon to them. In case of rain, we will not be able to see anything, so assemble the men in the theater and I will show them films of it."

The executive officer relayed the order to the adjutant:

"By order of the colonel, tomorrow at 2000 hours Halley's Comet will appear above the battalion area. If it rains, fall the men out in fatigues, then march them to the theater where this rare phenomenon will take place, something which occurs only once every seventy-five years."

The adjutant relayed the order to the commander:

"By order of the colonel, in fatigues at 2000 hours tomorrow evening, the phenomenal Halley's Comet will appear in the theater. In case of rain in the battalion area, the colonel will give another order, something which occurs once every seventy-five years."

The company commander passed the directive on to the first sergeant:

"Tomorrow at 2000 hours, the colonel will appear in the theater with Halley's Comet, something which happens every seventy-five years. If it rains, the colonel will order the comet into the battalion area."

The top sergeant's announcement in the formation next morning was:

"When it rains tomorrow at 2000 hours, the phenomenal seventy-five-year-old General Halley, accompanied by the colonel, will drive his Comet through the battalion theater in fatigues."

Learning to listen will require some hard work, but it's worth all the trouble.

Dump the fallacious ideas about listening!

A Critical Listening Incident

Someone begins to speak on a subject which does not particularly interest you. Do you—
   a. take a short nap?
   b. toy with the ideas presented and then discard them?
   c. walk away?
   d. listen attentively, hoping for some new idea you might adapt for your own use?

Answer: d. Definitely! More people are guilty of ignoring a speaker than they may realize. But if you discover you are one of them, do hasten to make amends. The perfect squelch is to have spoken and only been ignored.

18
Listening Inertia

As our ears are constantly bombarded by noise pollution, we develop, as a means of self-protection, a process I call "listening inertia," an internal squelching mechanism by which we automatically reject most of the sounds that come through our ears. —J.W.D.

The country of Brazil boasts the world's largest hydroelectric project at Itaipu; the Maracana, the world's largest soccer stadium which seats over 200,000 (without any adjoining parking space); the Amazon, the world's largest river; and what is claimed, without any exaggeration, to be the world's most beautiful city—Rio de Janeiro.

Surrounded by a lush tropical setting, with thirty-five miles of beaches and sandy coves, guarded from the sea by bold rock islands cropping out of the water, and located amidst soaring dramatic peaks, such as Sugar Loaf and the Hunchback (Corcovado), from which the most dramatic scenes in all the world may be viewed, Rio makes one more claim which the civic-minded say it could do without. When an international congress on acoustics was held in the city in 1980, Rio was officially given the dubious honor of being the world's noisiest city, with an average noise level of eighty-five decibels.

During a stay in the city I lived in a house, where, because of muggy heat and a temporary air conditioner failure, it was necessary to keep the windows open. Unfortunately the open windows also allowed the efforts of twelve youthful drummers to create, from 3:00 P.M. to midnight, the most earsplitting cacophony of jumbled sounds that ever came out of the jungle. I found it easy to believe that such drums, along with motorcycles and souped-up cars and sundry other noise sources have sent the official noise level over eighty-five decibels, and in districts like Copacabana, to an ear-shattering 100 decibels.

Small wonder a leading national newspaper pointed out that foreign visitors to the beautiful city are positively flabbergasted at the noise level, which they characterize as unbearable and harmful to the nerves. The newspaper called for what it termed "a guerrilla warfare against noise."

Auditory Insult

The noise level in Rio is only one example of what is happening to people today. While many are convinced of air pollution, which causes our eyes to water and is visible in the form of smog, we are generally not as aware of noise pollution. Noise pollution befouls our communication, threatens our health, and may even be related to our intelligence. A philosopher has said, "The amount of noise which anyone can bear undisturbed stands in inverse proportion to his mental capacity and may, therefore, be regarded as a pretty fair measure of it."

If this statement is true, we must be in grave danger of becoming a nation of half-wits, morons, and nincompoops, for never in our history have our delicate ears been assaulted with such a cacophony of deafening noise. We are victims of what has been called the auditory insult.

The unit most commonly used to measure sound is the decibel, named in honor of Alexander Graham Bell, famed inventor of the telephone. A decibel is defined as the faintest sound heard by the human ear. A steady noise of eighty-five decibels is considered safe, but the scale is logarithmic. An increase of ten decibels means a tenfold increase in sound intensity; twenty decibels, a hundredfold; and thirty decibels, a thousandfold increase. A misunderstanding of the scale gives rise to the fallacy that if eighty-five decibels is safe, then a person needn't worry about a slight increase to eighty-six or eighty-seven decibels. This is faulty reasoning.

We are victims of a noise attack wherever we go. Driving through the city, the level is eighty decibels, but passing the airport at the time of the jet aircraft takeoff exposes us to an incredible intensity of 140 decibels.

The U.S. Army has published a series of warnings to military personnel on the dangers to their ears of the noises they encounter in the course of their army service. For example, troops are warned about a 6000-pound fork lift, a 5000-pound dump truck, and a Huey helicopter; yet the noise of each of these is exceeded by many common household implements.

A man may flee the city's noise to the shelter of his home only to meet Junior and the lawn mower—which emits 107 decibels of sound. The noise level in the kitchen may become as high as 100 decibels. Everywhere in the modern home are noise-generating devices—blender, washer, dryer, vacuum cleaner, hair dryer—all polluting the air of the family domicile.

Adding to these radio, television, and stereo results in the ultimate cacophony, and it's getting worse all the time. A recent report out of Austin, Texas, claims overall loudness of environmental noise is doubling every decade.

The following chart lists common noise makers and their decibel levels:

Jet Plane	140
Pneumatic Riveter	130
Rock Music with Amplifiers (4-6 ft. away)	120
Power Mower (107)	110
Noisy Kitchen	100
Subway (inside)	90
City Traffic	80
Fortissimo Singer	70
Ordinary Conversation	60

Decibel Scale

Hearing or Listening?

William James spoke about his age as a megaphonic era. Today, such a description would be the understatement of the year.

Faced with these threats of noise pollution, we soon discover that the human body has defense mechanisms in the form of *nonlistening*. The experience may be highlighted by the use of the words *hearing* and *listening*. To the uninitiated these words may seem to be synonyms, but in actuality they are very different. *Hearing* describes the process whereby a sound wave travels through the air, hits the ear, is translated into neural current, and proceeds to the brain. *Listening* is the word which describes the sorting-out process by which we choose and decide which stimuli will have our attention.

The whole operation of a sound wave's transmission to the brain takes place with lightning speed. The brain itself is programmed by years of experience and conditioning to handle the auditory impressions it is fed. Like a busy executive's efficient secretary who sorts out the correspondence, keeping only the most important for his personal perusal, some sounds are summarily rejected, while other have total attention focused on them. This selective process of the brain is the main distinction between *hearing* and *listening*.

Internal Earplugs

Modern man cannot depend on ear guards like those jetliner ground crews wear as protection against the earsplitting sounds of the whining engines. Instead, most humans are in a lifelong process of gradually developing their own internal earplugs as protection against the constant acoustical bombardment of twentieth-century living.

For the first few nights after I moved to a house located near a railroad track, every passing train disturbed my sleep. But, as time went by, I grew less and less aware of the noise until a visitor inquired if the passing trains bothered me. I replied, "What trains?" My internal squelching mechanism had taken over so I no longer listened to the railroad noises.

There is obviously some wisdom in our natural tendency *not* to listen. Though the mechanism protects us in many ways, it also does us a disservice, by causing us to miss many of the things to which we should listen. A really observant person has to work hard to overcome listening inertia.

As Solomon said: "Don't talk so much. You keep putting your foot in your mouth. Be sensible and turn off the flow!" (Prov. 19:19 LB).

Attaining the Skill

Listening is not easy; it is one of the most difficult skills to master. My wife will vouch for this.

We had attended a conference in the course of which I had to make five presentations in one day. Following the evening event, we returned to the motel room, and I flopped into a comfortable chair and tried to recoup my dwindling energies.

"Why don't we go down to the coffee shop and have a dish of ice cream?" suggested my wife.

Filled with self-pity, I answered, "I can't be bothered. It's all right for you, but I'm worn out. I had to speak five times today!"

Quick as a wink my bright-eyed spouse rejoined, "Well, I had to *listen* five times today!"

She was right. Listening is often far more difficult than talking; and it requires determination, energy, and discipline to attain the skill.

A Critical Listening Incident

A guest begins to discuss something about which you happen to be better informed than he. Do you—
    a. announce your personal knowledge or experience on the subject and take over?
    b. say nothing of your own qualifications, but correct him on certain points as he is speaking?
    c. listen with interest and make some comment to show that interest when he is finished, but fail to mention that you know even more about it?

d. listen patiently. Then smile and remark, "Yes, I know. I have done research in that field myself for years"?

Answer: c. You have to be both generous and possessed of willpower not to steal a little thunder in situations like this, but you'll feel better for keeping mum. And you never gain, even in prestige, by deflating another.

19
Listening for the Sound of Silence

To be creatively silent calls for effort and self-discipline. —J.W.D.

The Chinese girl who sat on the front row of my classroom was the type of student for whom every teacher longs. She looked up with eager eyes, periodically writing in her notebook with great rapidity, giving the impression that she must catch every pearl of wisdom as it fell from the lecturer's lips.

As I remember it, there was only one occasion on which she did not give her wholehearted assent to everything I said. In fact, she let out a startled cry that temporarily disorganized the class.

While discussing the listening process, I had used Dominick Barbara's phrase and was exhorting my students to "listen for the sound of silence."

My favorite Oriental student exclaimed in painful dismay, "Sound of silence? How can silence have a sound?"

The expression which upset a girl already puzzled by the intricacies of the English language is really a paradoxical statement. It aims at dramatizing the difficulty of maintaining silence.

The Simplicity of Silence

It will probably horrify teachers of small children in religious schools when I express my doubts as to the validity of the thesis that God is easily discovered in the beauties of nature. In my visits to parts of the country noted for scenery, I have seldom been impressed by the depth of religious devotion of the inhabitants.

On the other hand, trips to the sandy plains of West Texas have sent me home pondering the religious dedication of so many people in those areas. Great numbers of crowded churches are located in country which would not be considered beautiful by many. I am sometimes tempted to claim there is an inverse ratio of religious devotion to natural beauty.

A good proportion of the great religions, including Judaism, Christianity, and Islam, either came into existence or were nurtured in the silent sands of the desert. Here it was that Moses saw the burning bush, Jesus overcame temptation, Muhammad had his vision, and Paul thought out the implications of his new-found faith.

Void of distraction, the desert provided the silent environment within which a man could clearly hear the voice of deity.

I sometimes smile when I hear ministers state the assumption that a new type of building will create a worshipful atmosphere. In my late adolescence I occasionally worshiped with the Plymouth Brethren. Meeting in the barest halls, adorned only with inartistic signs carrying Scripture verses, they had the most worshipful services I have ever attended.

Silence was the key to it all. No organist in whispered conferences, pushing or pulling stops, beamed smiling messages. Greeting, giggling, whispering, shuffling were all outlawed. Coughing was hushed by the miracle drug, reverence. Children were quieted. People tiptoed to their places in the circle to sit with bowed heads or read their Bibles. The keen anticipation of the movement of the Spirit of God in leading one of the assembled laymen to announce a hymn, read the Scripture, or offer prayer was sensed in these moments of deep reverence which contrasts sharply with the hubbub of many Protestant services. Their secret was the use of silence.

The Variety of Silence

All silence is not of equal value. The sound of silence brings a variety of messages and speaks with any of a number of voices.

- The *silence of retreat* is the sulking attitude which says, "All right, I'll just cut myself off from you and I'll wear you down by refusing to talk." This emotional curtain can isolate people as effectively as the Berlin Wall.
- If, by some chance, you imagine silence is passive, just wait until you encounter *defiant silence*. It fairly shouts and communicates the idea, "O.K., I am going to listen. Trot out your evidence. Let's hear if you can really tell me something." Answering defiant silence is like trying to recapture a parakeet that has escaped from its cage in a darkened room. The responder hardly knows where to go or what to do, with his subject determined to side-step and keep him in a blind stumble.
- The *silence of rebuke* is used effectively by a speaker who regularly addresses teen-agers

and is bothered when a couple of them start whispering to each other. As they commence to confer, he stops his speech, a deathly silence following. People begin to look uncomfortable as the culprits gradually understand, smile innocently, and gaze intently at the speaker. He takes up his talk again, having gained their attention with the silence of rebuke.

The Creativity of Silence

Creative silence says: "I could fill up the time with small talk, and there may even be something I could say which interests you. But that is not my purpose. I want to provide you with a situation in which you can think about yourself, your failures and shortcomings, problems, assets, and future plans. Because of my interest in you, I am willing to sit in silence with you."

Like any other creative activity, this type of silence calls for self-control and diligent practice. For most of us ten seconds of silence can seem like ten hours. The garrulous age in which we live has made us fearful of quietude. Life is too much a carnival of noise, when we really need a chapel of silence.

I once counseled a woman who told a story of her troubles with great difficulty, her rate of speaking gradually building, then slowing down as her agitation subsided. Like the calm following the storm, she lapsed into silence.

After what seemed an eternity, but was probably in fact only a few minutes, I asked, "Is there something else you would like to tell me?"

The woman was startled and confused. Later investigation proved she had been thinking furiously, and I had interrupted her train of thought.

Barbers, hairstylists, and other members of the hair-fixing fraternity are not generally known as a taciturn group. In fact, the image we have of them as a whole is of people with a reputation for being loquacious. Apparently, it was ever thus. The ancient Greeks told a story of the man who was asked by his talkative barber: "How would you like your hair cut?"

Quickly came the reply, "In silence."

Were I asked, "How should I go about counseling somebody?" I would repeat the words spoken to the Greek barber: "In silence."

Storytellers are casting their ancient spell in a comeback of their art. Much discussion takes place concerning the craft and skill of the raconteur. One unusual discovery is the strange effect that the telling of a story has upon the storyteller himself. As one describes his experiences he says, "the story tells you." These spinners of yarns have also discovered techniques that provide effective guidelines for communicators and counselors. Noting the tendency of many storytellers to maintain a constant flow of words, one practitioner points out that the art may be viewed as a type of music; the teller, the instrument. He counsels, "Be brave enough to use silence."

Rushing in to cover over the periods of silence may hold up the redemptive process of a troubled individual who may be building up his courage to make a clean breast of it all. Or he may be trying to put things together in a way that they can be expressed. He *needs* some quiet time in which to do his thinking.

A troubled man went to visit his physician with a list of anxieties and fears. The wise doctor told his patient to take a day off work and visit the beach. At the end of the consultation, the physician placed in his hand an envelope with instructions to open it when he reached his destination.

He found a quiet spot at the beach and opened the envelope. On a small piece of paper, he read the words, "Listen carefully." Later he told of the rewards of hearing for the first time in years the lapping of the waves, the song of the bird, and the sighing of the wind. He discovered that a moment of silence could be a moment of revelation.

"Silence is the element in which great things fashion themselves," said Carlyle.

Many professional psychotherapists have come to recognize the use of silence. Reik states the situation clearly, "In psychoanalysis . . . what is spoken is *not* the important thing. It appears to us more important to recognize what speech conceals and what silence reveals."

A Critical Listening Incident

You have nothing else pressing to do; but you are bored by the long drawn-out story that is being told. Do you—
 a. find something to divert your attention, such as a magazine, until it's over?
 b. listen with apparent animation, smiling and nodding encouragement?
 c. break in when you can, and change the subject?
 d. invent some excuse for escape—such as the telephone or a headache?

Answer: b. And try to be charitable about it. Remember, you yourself may sometimes talk far too long without being aware of it.

20

Asking Questions— Carefully

An imaginative question has universal appeal.
—J.W.D.

A group of men sat in a barbershop, gazing into space, each thinking his own thoughts and inwardly hoping his turn for tonsorial attention might soon arrive.

A smiling, bright-eyed youth entered, took his seat, and surveyed the zombies lining the wall.

After a few futile efforts to start a conversation, he addressed an outrageous question to the farthest barber: "How would you like to work on heads without bodies?"

The barber pondered the question a moment and chuckled. Some of the others looked up in amazement. At the end of the row, a customer, obviously anxious to get back to his work, interjected a thought: "Maybe they'll come up with an idea that will let people leave their heads at the shop while they continue their job at the office."

The sandy-haired youth in the center joined in: "Wouldn't it be fine if you could get a *spare* head?"

A man whose small edging of fluff around the periphery of baldness only barely justified his presence in the shop wistfully commented, "It might even be possible to trade in your old head on a new one."

In short order a stimulating conversation was underway. Strangers were talking, smiling, and laughing with one another.

The youth who had started it all sat quietly, smiling with satisfaction. He was now the listener.

The harrassed barbers who were trying to keep up with demands, and the longsuffering customers who were thinking of all they needed to do were equally ready to respond to an unusual question.

In the course of a presentation by outstanding clergyman Dr. Charles Allen, he told the audience he had developed a marvelous new counseling technique. Allen was already known for some of his good books, such as *God's Psychiatry* and *Twelve Ways to Solve Your Problems,* and the thought of a new technique caused his audience to listen even more intently.

Allen presented his counseling methodology in his own inimitable way. When someone came to him for counseling, he said, he would ask: "What seems to be your situation?" His counselee would then proceed to recount all the difficulties that he was facing, sometimes taking a considerable amount of time.

When at last this recital was ended, the astute clergyman would ask a second question: "What do you think you should do?" His client then advanced his ideas about the courses of action that he felt he needed to take, and by the time this plan of action had been presented, the time had come to end the counseling session.

As Allen saw it, two questions could handle the whole situation.

The Varieties of the Question

The questioning method is one of the oldest techniques known to educators. Just watch a skillful teacher at work and see the way in which questions are used.

Several types of questions can be effective in heart listening.

1. *Open questions* seek the help of the six words about which Rudyard Kipling wrote:

I keep six honest serving-men,
[They taught me all I knew]
Their names are What and Why and When
And How and Where and Who.

These "honest serving-men" invite someone to express his ideas on one of a variety of subjects. Examples: "*How* do you think your husband should go about handling this problem?" "*What* have you done about getting this matter under control?" "*Why* is this relationship so important to you?" "Tell me *how* your daughter's attitudes look to you."

2. *Now questions* cause the subject to become vividly aware of the moment when he has something special to contribute in response to the question.

The late President Kennedy was well known for his witty answers to questions fired at him. It is not such common knowledge that he also had a peculiar ability to ask an incisive question and pay unusual attention to the reply.

3. *Ask-for-help* questions comprise one of the most effective ways of establishing contact with a person. Women seem better equipped to use the help method than men.

My wife imagines the best way to find a correct route as we travel is to "ask somebody." I know, of course, that a map is all that I need.

As I am struggling with my map reading, she coyly suggests, "Why don't you ask somebody?"

I respond, "Honey, I have a perfectly good map prepared by the American Automobile Association. They ought to know. I really don't need any help."

And this is the way it goes on until I finally give in and ask, only to discover that I am miles out of my way and would have saved an hour if I had only asked *earlier.*

Although I have a built-in resistance to this method of automobile navigation and feel we should not bother any other person, our inquiries have always been graciously received, for there is nothing more appealing than someone who is seeking help.

"I need help. I have absolutely no knowledge about astronomy; yet I'd love to know something about satellites . . ." With words similar to these beamed at the subject's special knowledge, many a clammed-up individual has been persuaded to release his pearls of wisdom.

May I Help You?

An offer to be of assistance may also have a subtle magic. But it must be done sincerely. Reaching out a helping hand to a troubled person may easily open up a channel of communication.

I often talked at length with my grandfather. Nothing remarkable about that, you might think, but you obviously didn't know my granddaddy. A medium-sized, wrinkled, suntanned individual with a straight back, he wore a luxuriant crop of fascinating mutton-chop whiskers. He was, to put it mildly, a man of few words. Compared with him, Calvin Coolidge must have been a compulsive talker.

Addressed by most of the family as "Dah," a name whose origin was long ago lost, he was a hard worker who believed actions spoke louder than words. He seldom talked with his twelve children, evidently believing the provision of bread and lodging told the story.

Immediately following the stonily silent completion of supper, he saddled and mounted his horse, riding at a leisurely pace to the small country store where he sat in the corner and listened to the other farmers talk.

The only consistent sound I ever heard from him came after he had retired to his room. The victim of an asthmatic condition, he used some sort of atomizer device which puffed the misty medicine into his lungs with a hiss.

The sound from my hitherto silent relative mystified and fascinated me. I sometimes wondered if he were pumping himself up before sallying forth to work in the fields or visit the country store.

In my eleventh year, as always, we made our annual visit to my grandfather's farm. After a year in the city I was anxious to get down to the open fields where Grandpa was harvesting the alfalfa.

The aroma was *so* fragrant. My grandfather had cut the crop, and now he raked it away, piling it into heaps ready for pitching up onto the cart.

With boyish enthusiasm I greeted him, only to be answered by a noncommital grunt. Taking a breather on a shady side of the cart, he looked hot and tired. As he poured some water from a canvas waterbag into the tin cup, I felt sorry for him, so I asked, "Can I help you, Grandpa?"

He looked a little stunned at first, but half-nodded his permission. Anxious to work off the boredom of that long train ride, I gave all my boyish energy to taking up that lovely, sweet-smelling alfalfa. Later on, I climbed up on the cart while he pitched it up to me and I pushed it into the corners, jumping around as I had the time of my life.

From that day on we were the best of friends. One evening as we sat on the front porch of the farmhouse, he was peering at the newspaper through his magnifying glass, reading the advertisements. He addressed a rare question to me: "I wonder what them kippered snakes taste like?"

Puzzled at the thought of some enterprising company's putting snakes in cans, I walked over and looked at the paper. "Grandpa," I whispered, "that's kippered *snacks.*"

A rare smile lit his face as he patted my hand in a gesture of appreciation. After that he often asked me to check up on things not too clear to his aging eyes.

I felt very proud of my newfound position. I often rode with him on the farm cart. The other members of the family wondered at this strange relationship and why he should have chosen me to talk to.

One day my uncle, who was himself quite a talker, challenged Grandpa to explain why he talked only to *me.* Grandpa puffed on his pipe for a while before answering, "Maybe because he asked me if he could help me."

Just for Starters

The best conversation openers don't just seek out facts, but focus on the feelings of the subject, attempting to help him verbalize his emotional reactions, opinions, ideas.

One simple rule of thumb for opening conversation with question is never to ask a question which can be answered by yes or no unless you have a follow-up query ready.

You are talking with Joe Jones, who seems to be greatly troubled by some domestic problem.

One way of approaching his problem would be to ask him, "Do you like living with your brother?" The obvious answers are either yes or no, and after one or the other is given, looking at each other is about all there is left to do.

A better question would be, "How do you feel

about living with your brother?" This question may evoke his feelings and ideas and stimulate further helpful discussion.

Try out your powers of questioning. In the following list, some of the questions are good and some poor. Check ☑ the good ones, ☒ the poor ones.

1. Did you have a good day today? ☐
2. How do you feel about this? ☐
3. Do you like your work? ☐
4. Have you any ideas on the subject? ☐
5. "Oh, really?" ☐
6. Would you explain this to me? ☐
7. Will you accept the new offer? ☐
8. What is your reaction to this situation? ☐
9. Do you love me? ☐
10. Please give me your opinion on the subject. ☐

Questions 1, 3, 5, 7, 9 are poor because they can be answered with a noncommittal yes or no. Questions 2, 4, 6, 8, 10 are better, because they stimulate further conversation.

Questions With a Purpose

Writing under the heading, "Ask, Don't Tell," a writer concluded there were guidelines for effective questioning.

- Take every possible chance to ask a searching question, *then keep quiet.* (When you're talking, you're not learning anything.)
- One thoughtful question is worth a dozen inquisitive ones. The prod-and-pry approach makes people clam up.
- Questions that come close to the other person's true interest get the best answers—provided you are interested too.

- Be prepared to wait. Sometimes a long silence can be more rewarding than another question.
- *In every case,* the quality of an answer depends on the quality of attention given to the questioner.
- Questions must spring from honest inquiry, not from attempts at flattery or efforts to manipulate the other person's thinking.
- Questions that deal with a person's *feelings* are more provocative than tose that deal with *facts.*

Harry Emerson Fosdick, the celebrated preacher, was asked the secret of posing a good question. His reply was, "I suppose the secret, if there is one, is to realize that questioning and listening are inseparable. The asking of good questions represents listening on its highest plane, and that of course can never be faked or turned on—it must come from within. I believe it's the quality of attention that makes all the difference."

Ask a question—but do it carefully!

21
Avoiding Common Traps

We can be experts on details, gifted outguessers, skillful cross-examiners, or imaginative daydreamers—but we cannot at the same time be good listeners. —J.W.D.

If we are going to listen, we must pay attention! We should convey the impression that we are with the speaker every inch of the way.

Four possible traps into which the unwary listener may fall are: Keeping the record straight, outguessing the speaker, conducting a cross-examination, and wandering mentally from the subject. These are not the failures of the indifferent, but of the overly enthusiastic and inventive.

The Record-keeper

Because any conversation is carried on in some context, it is often necessary to have some background information about the events leading up to the experiences under discussion to give meaning to what is being related. Nevertheless there are people whose passion for correctness and detail will bog down any effort at conversation.

Listen to Sonya and Bryant Gilmore talking with a group of their friends. Bryant is telling of an unusual experience which befell the Gilmore family on their last vacation.

Sonya's eyes are gleaming as she too, in her imagination, recalls that remarkable adventure.

"We left about the middle of July," begins Bryant.

"Not really the middle, Honey," says his sweet little wife. "It was actually the twenty-seventh . . ."

"Was it really? You know, I thought it was about the fifteenth or sixteenth; in fact, I well remember that was the day Harry Jones borrowed the lawn mower . . ."

The story is half-ruined already. The listeners begin to wonder inwardly if the Gilmores will ever get to their trip.

Having failed to settle the date, Mr. Gilmore, just a little red in the face, plunges into his story, with Mrs. Gilmore hovering around to pounce on the next inaccuracy.

"We threw in our lines and in no time flat the fish were almost jumping into the boat. Within twenty minutes we had a big mess of fish. There must have been fifty fish on the string by the time we stopped!"

"Oh, Honey, you know there were only thirty-five."

"Thirty-five! Why, I caught twenty-five myself, and Johnny and Jimmy must have easily landed another twenty-five between them."

Mrs. Gilmore heaves a sigh and looks apologetically at the company. "That's my husband! Always multiplies the number by two to make it better."

Mr. Gilmore's annoyance index rises as the conversation continues. He finally glares at his wife and lapses into silence.

Mrs. G., having made sure that every minute detail is correct and now vaguely aware of her spouse's antagonism, finally decides to retire to the kitchen to prepare a snack.

What did it matter when they left for their vacation or how many fish they caught? These were side issues of no importance to their guests.

By insisting on the minutiae, Mrs. Gilmore had annoyed and frustrated her husband, embarrassed their visitors, and generally cast a shadow on the evening.

The Outguesser

I have a friend who is a real intellect—bright, quick, and sharp. I always used to delight in meeting her, but something strange happens when we begin to talk.

As the conversation proceeds, I get the funny feeling that I don't know my own mind. Committed to helping me, she never lets me complete a statement. She works so hard and is so enthusiastic that I sometimes feel like pleading, "Please, don't help me so much!"

I begin to tell her about my recent flight to New York. "I was running late as I set out to the airport and when I arrived . . ."

"You had to wait at the ticket counter."

"No, the ticket counter was O.K., but . . ."

With almost any subject we discuss, I begin the conversation, then she guesses what I am going to say next and tries to help. The biggest problem is that her guesses are generally *wrong*.

How I dread that familiar gleam she gets in her eye! That signal tells me she is about to take over.

I have pondered the problem of telling her about this unfortunate habit that characterizes her life. Some people are so easily hurt that it ruins a friendship. Should I continue to put up with Jean? Or should I speak up?

Then I realized my good-natured intervention might completely alter the course of her life. I could see her in a future day taking me to one side to murmur gratefully, "Thank you so much, John. If you hadn't been brave enough to tell me, I might have still been interrupting people."

I took her out to lunch—to Nieman-Marcus. We ate *her* favorite—frog legs; I cannot bear them myself. They might *taste* like chicken but I know they are not.

She relaxed in her chair. "Well, John, what was it you wanted to talk to me about?"

I swallowed hard, plucked up my courage, and launched into the supreme effort to change the whole style of Jean's personality.

"How do you feel about people who interrupt . . . ?"

"I think it is an awful thing for one person to interrupt another when he is speaking. Of course, it is different if you go to his rescue. If you really know some poor person is trying to say something and simply can't get it out, you have a moral obligation to help him . . ."

So, I am reduced to avoiding Jean. When I see her coming I sometimes wistfully think it would be nice to talk with her, but I just cannot bear to think of starting out on so many conversational journeys that will never be completed.

Don't try to outguess. You might be wrong . . .

The Cross-examiner

The cross-examiner is like the famous Sergeant Friday of television fame, whose oft-repeated statement was, "I only want the facts." These human fact-finders can slow down any conversation.

Visiting Pelican Island on the Indian River was a tremendous experience and privilege for me. We boarded an air boat and skimmed along inches above the water, watching pelicans rise from the island at our approach—a noisy, flapping cloud. Guided by the game warden, we peeped at nests and had eyeball contact with babies as big as eagles. We marveled at the ecological cycle of fish providing food for pelicans, who, in turn, fertilized the surrounding waters, causing the multiplication of marine life.

Ruth should be told about this, I thought. A member of the Audubon Society, an avid bird watcher, she would be the first person I'd contact when I arrived home.

Scarcely recovered from the trip, I picked up the phone and dialed Ruth's number.

"Ruth, this is John."

"Oh, hello, John."

"Ruth, I had a wonderful experience! While I was in Florida I took a trip in an air boat to Pelican Island and saw the one place where pelicans nest in great numbers."

"Were they white pelicans or brown pelicans?"

"I don't know."

"You don't know? Didn't your guide explain to you about the different types and colors?"

"Well, no, they all looked sort of dirty."

"The white pelican has a wing span of about nine feet; the brown, only about six feet. The white pelican flies with its head kind of hunched back. If it plunges into the water when seeking its food, it would be a brown pelican. On the other hand, if it were a white pelican, it would scoop up fish while it was swimming. Does that help you, John?"

"Er . . . yes. Oh, Ruth, there is someone at the door. Why don't I call you back later?"

Ruth's cross-examining had thoroughly demoralized me.

There is all the difference in the world between a district attorney's fighting for justice, struggling to get the truth out of a reticent criminal, and a person's trying to encourage a conversation with another. The subject is not likely to be an enthusiastic talker if he feels he is on trial for perjury or is being given an oral examination for a Ph.D. degree.

The Daydreamer

As we sit in an audience listening to a speaker, we may follow him for a short period. Then a picture of the office and work awaiting our attention flashes onto the screens of our minds. So we take a mental trip back to our desks, look over our correspondence, check up on our secretaries, and then rejoin the speaker.

A little later in the discourse the golf course begins to beckon, and off we go to bask in the warm sun, admire the condition of the green, and visit with old cronies. We visualize the beautiful drive, the flawless putt, our opponents' dismay, and the concluding moment of triumph.

But if, on one of these side journeys, we stay away too long, we may discover, on our return, that the speaker has gotten so far ahead that there is no chance of catching up. So we sink into a passive resignation, fasten a fixed look on our faces, and hope the speaker will soon tire and quit.

The good listener doesn't go on side excursions. He tries to anticipate where the speaker is going, moving out ahead like a scout on a wagon train. As soon as he realizes the speaker is going in another direction, he hurries back to rejoin him.

Fight back every urge to set the record straight, outguess the speaker, cross-examine the subject, or

Avoiding Common Traps / 171

make mental excursions. Make your choice instead to be a good listener.

A Critical Listening Incident

A friend of yours is one of those rambling conversationalists who starts a good story, but follows half a dozen byways before getting back to it. Do you—
    a. correct him when he misquotes a date or statistic?
    b. ask him for more details than he is able to supply?
    c. smile vacantly while planning the evening's menu?
    d. deftly attempt to steer him to home base by an eager question now and then, such as: "Yes, but what happened to the fish?" or, "I can't wait to hear what Mary said when you told her what was up . . ."?

Answer: d. In this case, an interruption, if tactfully spirited enough, will please the storyteller. People like to feel their listeners relish the tale enough to want to hear its outcome.

22
Be Sure to Catch the Balloons

Any sizable number of people who refuse to listen attentively to a speaker can transform an eloquent orator into a halting, hesitant, dry-as-dust bumbler. —J.W.D.

Public speaking may be thought of as launching balloons inscribed with messages printed in large letters. Each of these idea-balloons trails a long string, which would seem to make it simple for the listener to grasp it as it passes by.

While much of the speaker's ability lies in his capacity to make his idea-balloons attractive to his audience, the listeners' responsibility is just as important.

A prospective listener sits in an audience as the speaker releases his balloons and sends them floating across the room trailing their strings. As the balloons sail toward the listener, he is faced with the responsibility for three alternatives of action.

He may be bodily present but only partly conscious. In this state he is only vaguely aware of his surroundings. The idea-balloons drift lazily by, but he pays them scant attention, content to relax in the twilight zone of inattention.

Or perhaps, for a brief moment, he toys with the possibility of inspecting the balloons more closely. But they are not intriguing to him, and after a casual glance, he lets them drift on their way.

A third possibility is that the listener may examine the balloons carefully, noting their beauty. As the balloons come closer, he becomes more intent, enthralled with their potential. He searches his mind for associated ideas, reaches out, takes a firm grip on the strings, and gathers a colorful bunch. These new ideas are now his.

It is this third attitude that is a must for the listener.

An Active Listening Exercise

Try an exercise in listening. Listen to someone talking—a political or after-dinner speech, a sermon, or the story of some troubled person who wants to share it. Enter actively into the epxerience in the following ways:

- Start with a determination to overcome your listening inertia. Like the naval command, give yourself a strong and certain, "Now hear this!"
- Examine the facts as they are presented to try to determine if they are accurate or are just being presented to prove a point or bolster a case.
- Look for a message beyond the words. The changing tones and fluctuating facial expressions, gestures, and body movements all carry a message.

- The speaker may say something that you need to hear. Decide not to let prejudice block your appreciation and evaluation of the message.
- Fight distractions. Refuse to be lured away by your curiosity. Reject the incidentals, interruptions, and any peripheral activity.
- Try to anticipate where the speaker is going. Scout ahead. If he goes on another trail, retrace your steps and rejoin him.
- Focus your attention on the theme or main message. See how other material bolsters this basic idea.
- Make periodic mental summaries so that you know where you've been and have a launching pad for what follows.
- Underline the illustrations and examples. They will become easily remembered reference points.

This exercise may be valuable in many ways. Listening will become much more interesting and rewarding. You may even discover another bonus.

When I first became interested in listening, I began to research the books I felt would contain the information I needed. Naturally I turned to the extensive literature of psychology and psychotherapy, but there was little to be found. Then I unearthed an unexpected wealth of information in books on speech.

The authorities in the field of speech realized early that a student must first of all learn to listen in order to become a good speaker. As we learn to listen, we may find we have unwittingly grasped the principles of good expression, ending up as a speaker to whom other people will want to listen.

Half the Secret

Make no mistake about it: A listening audience is more than half the secret of any successful speech.

To be effective listeners, we must give the speaker our undivided attention. It is his moment, and every aspect of our demeanor must say: "Come on. Let's have it. You're in the center of the stage of my thinking."

The good listener doesn't do a lot of things. He cannot lean back in his chair with eyes half-closed as if he were taking an afternoon nap or dart furtive looks as if mentally cataloging the books on his shelves. He doesn't steal glances at his watch with the inference: "Time is up; you've been here long enough." He won't doodle on a pad as though preparing notes for a speech of his own.

The good listener is relaxed. The telephone is cared for; his secretary, warned against interruptions. He leans slightly toward the speaker, his eyes focused on him, not in a staring match, but in a coaxing, interested manner. Every aspect of the listening one says, "Tell me more."

Can Anyone Hear Me?

A lady from North Carolina was surely glad that somebody was listening when she found herself in the most difficult situation of her life. Her husband, an enthusiastic flier, had been licensed to pilot light planes for some thirteen years. Though his wife didn't care much about flying, when he urged her to come with him one Sunday afternoon, she reluctantly agreed. The mechanics of flying had never appealed to her, and she admitted that she had never even closed the door of the plane by herself.

After an uneventful check of the plane and takeoff, her husband set a course for an airport about eighty miles away. However, not far into the flight, he noted the possibility of rain and decided they should return to their home base. Then suddenly he shivered a little, said, "I feel faint," and slumped forward in his seat. His wife, first believing that he was pretending, realized that he had experienced a heart attack, and had died instantly. His now lifeless body slumped down in the seat beside her. Her heart pounded with the realization that, bereft of flying knowledge, she was sharing the plane with a dead pilot.

Moving through the sky, 3500 feet above the ground, the lady reached over, picked up the microphone the way she had seen her husband do many times before, pressed the button, and sent out her urgent message: "Is anybody listening? Is anybody listening? Please, somebody help me! My husband has collapsed and I do not know how to fly a plane!"

Anyone who has worked with any type of radio transmitter knows that transmitting a message into the air waves is an act of faith. The message has gone out, but is anyone tuned to this frequency? If they are, will they respond?

It so happened *many* people were listening when the lady transmitted her desperate message. The air waves crackled with instructions as pilots and air controllers tried to pinpoint her whereabouts and advise the "lady in distress," as she was now known and addressed. The result was utter confusion. Heard clearly above the chaos was one calm, reassuring voice: "Ma'am, I am an instructor . . . and I am going to tell you how to fly that plane."

The pilot then proceeded to give a flying lesson to someone he could not see. He told her how to steer and how to keep the plane level, where to look for the throttle, and what dials to read. With care and precision he finally guided her to a safe landing at the airport.

Recalling her experience in an interview, the lady said, "It's a miracle that I landed that plane." And referring to the man who had guided her down to the landing strip, she could only marvel, "There's no question in my mind that God sent him."

For the student of listening, two considerations present themselves.

The first is that what happened to these two people physically is what happens to so many other people psychologically. It is typical of the dilemma of many people in the total situation of their lives that they are desperately and sometimes silently asking the question: "Is anybody listening?"

The second perspective is that there is a voice that is speaking to us in our need. The question is: "Will we hear?" The great statement of faith the Jewish people call the Shema (Deut. 6:4–9) begins with "O Israel, listen" (LB) and the listening theme continues through the Bible. In a time of low spiritual ebb, the Bible tells us "the word of the Lord was seldom heard" (1 Sam. 3:1 NEB). It seemed the problem was that no one was listening. Finally, a small boy responded, "Speak; thy servant hears thee" (1 Sam. 3:10 NEB) and the word of revelation came to him.

Listening for the Voice of God

When George Washington Carver, famous black scientist, appeared before a committee of the Congress, he was asked how he had made so many remarkable discoveries about horticulture. His response was: "I get up early in the mornings, and I go out into the woods and listen for the voice of God."

If we learn to listen, all sorts of things will happen. We will become better husbands, better wives, better family members, better employers, better supervisors. But, preeminently, if we learn to *really* listen, it may be said of us—as it was of one in a bygone day—"And thine ears shall hear a word behind thee, saying, This is the day, walk ye in it" (Isa. 30:21). If we hear *this* voice we are blessed indeed.